AT WIT'S END

AT WiT'S ENd

ERMA bombeck

ILLUSTRATED BY LORETTA VOLLMUTH

DOUBLEDAY & COMPANY, INC., GARDEN CITY, NEW YORK

LIBRARY OF CONGRESS CATALOG CARD NUMBER 67–19068
COPYRIGHT © 1965, 1966, 1967 BY NEWSDAY, INC.

CONTENTS

This isn't a book.

It's a group therapy session.

It is based on six predictable depression cycles that beset a woman during a twelve-month span.

These chapters will not tell you how to overcome these depression cycles.

They will not tell you how to cope with them.

They will have hit home if they, in some small way, help you to laugh your way through while hanging on to your sweet sanity.

AT WIT'S END

January 2 — March 4

what's a nice girl like me doing in a dump like this?

IT HITS on a dull, overcast Monday morning. I awake realizing there is no party in sight for the weekend, I'm out of bread, and I've got a dry skin problem. So I say it aloud to myself, "What's a nice girl like me doing in a dump like this?"

The draperies are dirty (and will disintegrate if laundered), the arms of the sofa are coming through. There is Christmas tinsel growing out of the carpet. And some clown has written in the dust on the coffee table, YANKEE GO HOME.

It's those rotten kids. It's their fault I wake up feeling so depressed. If only they'd let me wake up in my own way. Why do they have to line up along my bed and stare at me like Moby Dick just washed up onto a beach somewhere?

"I think she hears us. Her eyelids fluttered."

"Wait till she turns over, then everybody cough."

"Why don't we just punch her and ask her what we want to know."

13

"*Get him out of here.*"

"She's pulling the covers over her ears. Start coughing."

I don't know how long it will be before one of them discovers that by taking my pulse they will be able to figure out by its rapid beat if I am faking or not, but it will come. When they were smaller, it was worse. They'd stick their wet fingers into the opening of my face and whisper, "You awake yet?" Or good old Daddy would simply heave a flannel-wrapped bundle at me and say, "Here's Mommy's little boy." (Any mother with half a skull knows that when Daddy's little boy becomes Mommy's little boy, the kid is so wet he's treading water!) Their imagination is straight from the pages of Edgar Allan Poe. Once they put a hamster on my chest and when I bolted upright (my throat muscles paralyzed with fright) they asked, "Do you have any alcohol for the chemistry set?"

I suppose that's better than having them kick the wall until Daddy becomes conscious, then ask, "Do you want the cardboards that the laundry puts in your shirts?" Any wrath beats waking Daddy. There has to be something wrong with a man who keeps resetting his alarm clock in the morning and each time it blasts off smacks it silent and yells, "No one tells me what to do, Buddy."

Personally I couldn't care less what little games my husband plays with his alarm clock, but when I am awakened at 5:30, 6:00, 6:15, and 6:30 every morning, I soon react to bells like a punchy fighter. That's what I get for marrying a nocturnal animal. In the daylight, he's nothing. He has to have help with his shoelaces. In all the years we've been married he only got up once of his own accord before 9:30. And then his mattress was on fire. He can't seem to cope with daytime noises like flies with noisy chest colds, the crash of marshmallows as they hit the hot chocolate, the earsplitting noises milk makes when you pour it over the cereal.

The truth of it is, he's just not geared to function in an eight-to-five society. Once he even fell out of his filing cabinet.

Around eleven at night a transformation takes place. He stretches and yawns, then his eyes pop open and he kicks me in the foot and says, "What kind of a day did you have?"

"You mean we're still on the same one?" I yawn.

"You're not going to bed already, are you?"

"Yes."

"Would it bother you if I played the guitar?"

"Yes."

"Well, then maybe I'll read a little before I go to sleep."

"Why not? I have the only eyelids in the neighborhood with a tan."

No doubt about it, if I could arise in a graceful manner, I could cope.

It's starting to snow. Thanks a lot up there.

Before moving to the suburbs, I always thought an "Act of God" was a flash of lightning at Mt. Sinai or forty days and forty nights of rain. Out here, they call a snowfall an "Act of God" and they close the schools.

The first time it happened I experienced a warm, maternal glow, a feeling of confidence that I lived in a community which would put its children above inclement weather. The second time, that same week, I experienced a not-so-warm glow, but began to wonder if perhaps the kids could wear tennis rackets on their feet and a tow rope around their waists to guide them. On the third day school was canceled within a two-week period, I was organizing a dog-sled pool.

We racked up fifteen Acts of God that year and it became apparent to the women in our neighborhood that "somebody up there" was out to get us.

It got to be a winter morning ritual. We'd all sit around the radio like an underground movement in touch with the free world. When the announcer read the names of the schools closed, a rousing cheer would go up and the kids would scatter. I'd cry a little in the dishtowel, then announce

15

sullenly, "All right, don't sweat in the school clothes. RE-PEAT. Don't sweat in the school clothes. Hang them up. Maybe tomorrow you'll visit school. And stay out of those lunch boxes. It's only eight-thirty." My words would fall on deaf ears. Within minutes they were in full snow gear ready to whip over to the school and play on the hill.

Little things began to bother me about these unscheduled closings. For example, we'd drive by the school and our second-grader would point and ask, "What's that building, Daddy?" Also, it was March and they hadn't had their Christmas exchange yet. Our ten-year-old had to be prompted with his alphabet. And the neighborhood "Love and Devotion to Child Study" group had to postpone their meetings three times because they couldn't get the rotten kids out from under foot.

"We might as well be living in Fort Apache," said one mother. "If this snow doesn't melt soon, my kid will outgrow his school desk."

We all agreed something had to be done.

This year, a curious thing happened. In the newspaper it was stated that snow was no longer to be considered an Act of God by the state board of education. Their concern was that the children spend a minimum number of hours in school each week and that the buses would roll come yells or high water.

Snow is a beautiful, graceful thing as it floats downward to the earth, and is enhanced greatly by the breathtaking indentation of school bus snow tires. Snow is now considered an Act of Nature in the suburbs. And everyone knows she's a Mother and understands these things.

"Whip it up, group. Everyone to the boots!"

"What do you mean you're a participle in the school play and you need a costume? You be careful in that attic, do you

16

hear? If you fall through and break your neck, you're going to be late for school!"

A drudge. That's all I am. They'll all be sorry when I'm not around to run and fetch.

"So you swallowed the plastic dinosaur out of the cereal box. What do you want me to do, call a vet?"

Lunches. Better pack the lunches. Listen to them bicker. What do they care what I pack? They'd trade their own grandmother for a cough drop and a Holy picture.

Of course, none of these things would bother me if I had an understanding husband. Mother was right. I should have married that little literature major who broke out in a rash every time he read Thoreau. But no, I had to pick the nut standing out in the driveway yelling at the top of his voice, "I am thirty-nine years old. I make fifteen thousand dollars a year. I will not carry a Donald Duck thermos to the of-fice!" Boy, he wouldn't yell at me if my upper arms weren't flabby. He never used to yell at me like that. *He* should worry. He doesn't have to throw himself across the washer during "spin" to keep it from walking out of the utility room. He doesn't have to flirt with a hernia making bunk beds. He doesn't have to shuffle through encyclopedias before the school bus leaves to find out which United States president invented the folding chair.

It's probably the weather. "Everybody out!"

Look at 'em stumbling around the driveway like newborn field mice. It's the weather all right. No leaves on the trees. No flowers. No green grass. Just a big picture window with nothing to look at but . . . *a new bride moving into the cul-de-sac!* Well, there goes the neighborhood. Would you look at her standing at her husband's elbow as he stencils their marvy new name on their marvy new garbage cans? I suppose tomorrow she'll be out waxing her driveway. So give her a few years, and she'll be like the rest of us sifting through the coffee grounds looking for baby's pacifier.

17

What am I saying? Give her a few years of suburban living and she'll misplace the baby! What was it I was supposed to look for this morning? Maybe I'll think of it. I wonder how much time I waste each day looking for lost things. Let's see, I spent at least two hours yesterday looking for the bananas and enough straight pins to pin up a hem. Lucky the kids came up with the idea of walking across the floor in my bare feet or I'd be looking for pins yet. I suppose I could've uncovered the bananas by smelling breaths, but you have to trust someone sometime when they say no.

The day before that I misplaced the car keys. Of course, that's not my fault. That was the fault of the clown who left them in the ignition. You'd certainly never think to look there for them. Just say I spend about two hours a day looking for stuff. That amounts to 730 hours a year, not counting the entire months of November and December when I look for the Christmas cards I buy half price the preceding January.

I'd have a child growing up on the Pennsylvania Turnpike today if a group of picnickers hadn't noticed her sifting through trash barrels in the roadside park and become curious about how she got there. I wonder if other women piff away all that time looking for nail files and scotch tape.

I knew a woman once who always said, "Have a place for everything and everything in its place." I hated her. I wonder what she would say if she knew I rolled out of bed each morning and walked to the kitchen on my knees hoping to catch sight of a lost coin, a single sock, an overdue library book or a boot that could later inspire total recall.

I remember what I was going to look for . . . my glasses! But that was only if I wanted to see something during the day. So what do I have to see today that I couldn't put off until tomorrow? One of the kids said there was something strange in the oven. Probably a tray of hors d'oeuvres left over from the New Year's party. I'll look for the glasses tomorrow.

18

In the meantime, maybe I'll call Phyllis and tell her about the new bride. Better not chance it. Phyllis might be feeling great today and then I'd feel twice as crumby as I feel now.

This place will have to be cleaned before they can condemn it. Wouldn't be at all surprised if I ended up like my Aunt Lydia. Funny, I haven't thought about her in years. Grandma always said she ran away with a vanilla salesman. Lay you odds she made her move right after the holidays. Her kids probably hid the Christmas candy in the bedroom closet and the ants were coming out of the woodwork like a Hessian drill team. One child was going through the dirty clothes hamper trying to retrieve her "favorite" underwear to wear to school.

Lydia spotted her nine-year-old dog (with the Christmas puppy plumbing) and ran after it with a piece of newspaper. The dog read a few of the comics, laughed out loud, then wet on the carpet.

Uncle Wally probably pecked her on the cheek with all the affection of a sex-starved cobra and said he wanted to talk about the Christmas bills when he came home.

She passed a mirror and noticed a permanent crease on her face where the brush roller had slipped. Her skirt felt tight. She sucked in her breath. Nothing moved. Her best friend called to tell her the sequin dress she bought for New Year's Eve had been reduced to half price.

Speculating on her future she could see only a long winter in a house with four blaring transistor radios, a spastic washer, and the ultimate desperation of trying to converse with the tropical fish.

You know something. The odds are Aunt Lydia didn't even know the vanilla salesman. When he knocked on the door, smiled and said, "Good morning, madam, I'm traveling through your territory on my way to Forked Tongue, Iowa," Aunt Lydia grabbed her satchel, her birdcage, and her nerve elixir, closed the door softly behind her and said quietly, "You'll do."

Each woman fights the doldrums in her own way. This illustrated guide, *What to Do Until the Therapist Arrives with the Volleyball*, is not unique. Its suggestions may, however, keep you from regressing into a corner in a foetal position with your hands over your ears.

A: KNIT. Learning how to knit was a snap. It was learning how to stop that nearly destroyed me. Everyone in the house agreed I was tense and needed to unwind. So, I enrolled in an informal class in knitting.

The first week I turned out thirty-six pot holders. I was so intent on an afghan you'd have thought I was competing with an assembly line of back-scratcher makers from Hong Kong.

I couldn't seem to stop myself. By the end of the first month of knitting, I was sick from relaxation. There were deep, dark circles under my eyes. My upper lip twitched uncontrollably. There were calluses on both my thumbs and forefingers. I cried a lot from exhaustion. But I was driven

20

by some mad, inner desire to knit fifteen toilet tissue covers shaped like little men's hats by the end of the week.

In the mornings I could hardly wait until the children were out of the house so I could haul out my knitting bag full of yarn and begin clicking away. "All right, group, let's snap it up," I'd yell. "Last one out of the house gets underwear for Christmas."

"It's only six-thirty," they'd yawn sleepily.

"So you're a little early," I snapped impatiently.

"BUT IT'S SATURDAY!" they chorused.

My husband was the first one to suggest I needed professional help. "You've gone beyond the social aspect of knitting," he said. "Let's face it. You have a problem and you're going to have to taper off. From here on in no more yarn." I promised, but I knew I wouldn't keep my word.

My addiction eventually led to dishonesty, lying, cheating, and selling various and sundry items to support my habit. I was always being discovered. The family unearthed a skein of mohair in a cereal box and an argyle kit hidden in the chandelier, and one afternoon I was found feverishly unraveling an old ski cap just to knit it over again. One night when the clicking of the needles in the darkness awakened my husband, he bolted up in bed, snapped on the light, and said quietly, "Tomorrow, I'm enrolling you in 'Knitters Anonymous.' Can't you see what's happening to you? To us? To the children? You can't do this by yourself."

He was right, of course. "Knitters Anonymous" pointed out the foolishness of my compulsion to knit all the time. They eventually weaned me off yarn and interested me in another hobby—painting.

Would you believe it? I did eight watercolors the first week, fifteen charcoal sketches the second and by the end of the month I will have racked up twenty-three oils . . . all on stretched canvasses!

B: DRINK. A while back some overzealous girl watcher noted a mass migration of the Red-Beaked Female Lush to split-levels in the suburbs.

That a total of 68 percent of the women today drink, there is no quarrel. But that they've all settled in the suburbs is questionable. Following this announcement, we in the suburbs called an emergency meeting of the "Help Stamp Out Ugly Suburban Rumors" committee. We decided to dispel the stigma once and for all by conducting a sobriety test among women at 8 A.M. Monday morning in the town hall.

We uncorked—rather, uncovered—only three sherry breaths, a cognac suspect, and one woman who wasn't sauced at all but who said she always shook that way after getting her four kids onto the school bus in the mornings.

A few of them admitted to nipping away at a bottle of vanilla in the broom closet or getting a little high sniffing laundry bleach, but most of them confessed drinking in the suburbs is not feasible. They cited the following reasons.

Privacy: "You show me a mother who slips into the bathroom to slug down a drink and I'll show you seven children hidden in the bathtub flashing a Popeye home movie on her chest."

Discretion: "To children, drinking means an occasion.

22

When not given a satisfactory occasion to tout, they will spread it all over the neighborhood that Mama is toasting another 'No Baby Month.'"

Guilt: "With the entire block of my friends feeling trapped, bored, neurotic, and unfulfilled, why should I feel good and alienate myself?"

One woman did confess her system of rewarding herself with a drink had gotten a bit out of hand. At first she rewarded herself with a drink for washing down the kitchen walls or defrosting the refrigerator. Now she was treating herself to a drink for bringing in the milk or opening the can of asparagus at the right end.

Undoubtedly the girl watcher was tabulating the many gourmet clubs that have sprouted up in the suburbs. They are the harmless little luncheons where a light wine is served before the luncheon and gourmet foods using brandies and wines are served to stimulate women's interest in cookery.

Some of these are held on a monthly basis to observe some special occasion such as a birthday or an anniversary of a member. In our group, we also observe Mao Tse-tung's backstroke victory, the anniversary of the escape of Winnie Ruth Judd, the January White Sale at Penguin's Department Store, the introduction of soy beans to Latin America, and the arrival and departure dates of the *Queen Mary.* Each month we present an award to the most unique dish served. Last month's prize was copped by my neighbor for a wonderful dessert which consisted of a peach seed floating recklessly in a snifter of brandy.

Frankly I think the girl watchers owe the women of the suburbs an apology for their accusations. Anyone here want to drink to that?

c: READ. One of the occupational hazards of housewifery and motherhood is that you never get the time to sit down and read an entire book from cover to cover.

A spot check of my most erudite friends revealed that the

23

last books they read were: *Guadalcanal Diary*, *The Cat in the Hat Dictionary*, *The Picture of Dorian Gray*, and *First Aid*. (The fifth fell asleep over her "Know Your Steam Iron Warranty and Manual," but we counted it anyway.)

This is a sad commentary on the women who are going to be the mothers of all these scientists and skilled technicians of tomorrow. As I always say, "What doth it profiteth a woman to have a clean house if she thinks anthropologist Margaret Mead is a foot doctor!" (I recommended her to three of my friends.)

First, to find the right book. When you live in a small town you have to be pretty discreet about the books you check out. I, for one, don't want to be known behind the stalls as "Old Smutty Tongue." On the other hand, I don't want to spend my precious time plowing through *Little Goodie Miss Two Shoes and Her Adventures on Bass Island*.

"You know me pretty well, Miss Hathcock," I said to the librarian. "What book would you suggest for me?"

"*Sex and the Senior Citizen* with a glossary in the front listing all the pages with the dirty parts in boldface type," she answered crisply.

24

"Now, now, Miss Hathcock. We will have our little humor, won't we? Keep in mind I have very little time for reading and I want a book I can talk about in mixed company."

"If I were you," she said slowly, "I'd check out *Come Speed Read with Me* by M. Fletcher. It guarantees that in three days it will increase your reading speed enormously. You will be literally digesting an entire newspaper in nineteen minutes, novels in thirty minutes, and anthologies in an hour."

I tested myself the minute I got home. It took me forty-five minutes to read one paragraph. Maybe it was possible I had lost my old power of concentration. According to the contents of the first chapter, my diagnosis was a simple one. My eyes jerked and stopped at every word. I read each word, not sentences or images. That would take work.

Whenever I got the chance I picked up my *Come Speed Read with Me* book and spent an hour or two in diligent application.

Yesterday I approached Miss Hathcock at the return desk. "Well, how did your speed reading go?" she smiled. "Are you ready for the complete works of Churchill? How about *Hawaii*? Or Ted Sorensen's *Kennedy*?"

"Actually," I giggled, "I kept drowsing over chapter two. That's the 'Lack of Attention' chapter. Once I hurdle that, I feel I can whip through the entire thing in no time at all. How about an additional twenty-one days renewal on it?"

"How about *Sex and the Senior Citizen*?" she sighed wearily. "And I'll wrap it in a plain piece of brown paper."

D: TELEPHONE. A noted heart specialist has openly attacked women's use of the extension phone. He has charged these convenient outlets will (a) broaden hips, (b) cause sluggish circulation, and (c) eventually take away her lead over men in life expectancy.

Doctor, you are either naïve on the subject of telephone conditioning or you are pulling our fat, muscular legs.

25

At the first ring of the telephone, there is an immediate conditioned response that has every kid in the house galloping to the instrument to answer it. You show me a woman who is alert and who wears deep-tread sneakers and I'll show you a woman who gets to answer her own telephone.

Once Mama is settled comfortably on the phone, the children swing into action like a highly organized army on maneuvers, each marching to his favorite "No, No, Burn Burn" or whatever. Refrigerator doors pop open, cupboards bang back and forth, makeshift ropes carry kids sailing through the air, razor blades appear, strange children come filing through the doors and windows, the aromas of nail polish and gasoline permeate the air, and through it all one child will crawl up on the television set and take off his clothes! There is nothing like it to pep up tired blood.

Some mothers are clickers—that is, rather than interrupt a telephone conversation they will click fingers and point, pound on the table and point, whistle through their fingers and point, or pick up a club and point. So much for circulation.

Other mothers resort to muffled cries as they hold their hands over the receivers. They can't fake it. They've got to administer the whack, clean up the sugar, blow up a balloon, put out the fire, mop up the water *right now!* So much for hip exercises.

A few telephone exponents are a study in pantomime. I used to be mesmerized by a woman who formed the words, "I'm going to give you kids one in a minute," followed shortly by, "I'm going to give you kids two in a minute." She alone knew the magic number whereby she would stop and give them a belt.

Some mothers have even attempted to put a busy box, filled with toys, near their telephones. Of course, kids are too bright to fall for that. You could have Mary Poppins hanging by her umbrella whistling "Dixie" and kids would still roll the onions across the floor and gargle the laundry bleach.

I don't think women outlive men, Doctor. It only seems longer.

Shape Up Before You Ship Out

IN THE throes of a winter depression cycle, there is nothing that will set you off like a group of fashion authorities who want to know, "Is your figure ready for a bikini this summer?"

I got a flash for you, Charlie. My figure wasn't ready for a bikini last summer. Very frankly, I've hit a few snags.

You see, for years I have built my figure on the premise that "fat people are jolly." I have eaten my way through: pleasant, cheery, sunny, smiling, gay, spirited, chipper, vivacious, sparkling, happy, and sportive and was well on my way to becoming hysterical. Now I find that a group of experts say this is a myth. "Fat people aren't jolly at all. They're just

27

frustrated and fat." You'd have thought they would have said something while I was back on pleasant.

There was a time when I had a twenty-three-inch waist. I was ten years old at the time. As I recall, my measurements were 23-23-23. I'm no fool. Even at ten years, I knew I could never be too jolly with those figures so I started to eat.

In high school I used to reward myself with after-school snacks for (a) not stepping on a crack in the sidewalk, (b) spelling Ohio backwards, (c) remembering my locker combination.

After marriage, I added thirty pounds in nine months, which seemed to indicate I was either pregnant or going a little heavy on the gravy. It was the former. I am listed in the medical records as the only woman who ever gained weight *during* delivery.

My husband, of course, used to try to shame me by pasting a picture of Ann-Margret on the refrigerator door with a terse note, "Count Calories."

28

He hasn't tried that routine, however, since our trip to the shopping center last spring that coincided with a personal appearance by Mr. Universe.

"I thought we came here to look at a bedroom rug," he snapped. "You see one muscle, you've seen them all," he snorted.

"I've been married eighteen years and I've yet to see my first one," I said standing on my tiptoes. "Just let me see what he looks like."

Mr. Universe worked in a fitted black T-shirt and shorts. If muscles ever go out of style he could always get a job on the beach kicking sand in the faces of ninety-seven-pound weaklings and yelling, "Yea, skinny!" He thumped onto the platform and my jaw dropped.

"For crying out loud, close your mouth," whispered my husband. "You look like someone just dropped a bar bell on your foot."

"Did you ever see so many muscles in your life?" I gasped. "That T-shirt is living on borrowed time. And listen to that. He says it just takes a few minutes a day to build a body like his. Hey, now he's touching his ear to his knees. Can you touch your ear to your knee?"

"What in heaven's name for?" he sighed. "There's nothing to hear down there. Besides, I'd be embarrassed to look like that. My suits wouldn't fit right. And I couldn't bear having all those people staring."

"You're really sensitive about all this, aren't you?"

"I certainly am not," he said emphatically. "It's just that I'm not a beach boy."

"I'll say you're not a beach boy. Remember when that kid wanted to borrow your inner-tube last summer at the pool and you weren't wearing one?"

"Are we going to look at that bedroom rug or aren't we?" he growled.

"Not until you admit that you can't kick seven feet high,

throw a football seventy-five yards and jump over an arrow you're holding in both hands."

"Okay, so I'm not Mr. Universe."

"Then you'll take that picture of Ann-Margret off my refrigerator door?"

"Yes. You know, in my day I used to have a set of pretty good arm muscles. Here, look at this. I'm flexing. Hurry up! See it? How's that for muscle?"

Personally I've seen bigger lumps in my cheese sauce, but when you've won a war, why mess around with a small skirmish?

I think the trouble with most women dieters is that they can't get from Monday to Tuesday without becoming discouraged. I am a typical Monday dieter. Motivated by some small incident that happens on a Sunday ("Mama's outgrown her seat belt. We'll have to staple her to the seat covers, won't we?") I start in earnest on a Monday morning to record my era of suffering.

Diary of a Monday Dieter

8:00 A.M.: This is it. Operation twenty pounds. Called Edith and told her what I had for breakfast. Reminded her to read a story in this month's *Mother's Digest,* "How Mrs. M., St. Louis, ate 25 Hungarian Cabbage Rolls a Day and Belched Her Way to a Size 10."

12:30 P.M.: Forced myself to drink a cup of bouillon. Called Edith and told her I noticed a difference already. I don't have that stuffed feeling around my waist. I have more energy and my clothes fit better. Promised her my gray suit. After this week, it will probably hang on me like a sack.

4:00 P.M.: An article in *Calorie* (the magazine for people who devour everything in sight) offers a series of wonderful dinner menus for weight-watchers.

30

As I was telling Edith a few minutes ago, we mothers have an obligation to our families to feed them nutritious, slimming meals. Tonight we are having lean meat, fresh garden peas, Melba thins in a basket, and fresh fruit.

4:30 P.M.: Husband called to say he'd be late for dinner. Fresh garden peas looked a little nude, so added a few sauteed mushrooms and a dab of cream sauce. After all, why should the children be sick and suffer because they have a strong-willed mother?

4:45 P.M.: I ate the Melba toast—every dry, tasteless crumb of it! (Come to think of it the basket is missing.) Luckily I had a biscuit mix in the refrigerator and jazzed it up with a little shredded cheese and butter. The magazine said when you begin licking wax from the furniture you should supplement your diet with a snack.

5:00 P.M.: Well, maybe that lousy fruit in the bowl would look pretty good to Robinson Crusoe, but I put it under a pie crust where it belongs. In fifty minutes I'll have a warm cobbler, swimming in rich, thick cream. Who does my husband think he is? Paul Newman?

5:30 P.M.: The kids just asked what I am doing. I'm putting on a few potatoes to go with the gravy, that's what I'm doing. That's the trouble with kids today. Half of the world goes to bed hungry and they expect me to pour good meat drippings down the drain. Kids are rotten. They really are.

6:00 P.M.: Blood pressure has dropped. Stomach is beginning to bloat. Vision is impaired. I've added two more vegetables and a large pizza with everything to the menu. That fink Edith had the nerve to call and ask if she could have the blouse to the gray suit. Edith's a nice girl, but she's a pushy

31

individual who drives you crazy phoning all the time. I told the kids to tell her I couldn't talk. I was listening to my Bonnie Prudden records.

6:30 P.M.: Husband arrived home. I met him at the door and let him have it. If it weren't for his rotten working hours, I could be the slip of the girl he married. He had the gall to act like he didn't know what I was talking about.

No, I don't think I'm ready for a bikini again this year. Heaven knows I try to bend to the dictates of fashion, but let's face it, I'm a loser. When I grew my own bustle, they went out of style. When my hips reached saddlebag proportions, the "long, lean look" came in. When I ultimately discovered a waistline, the straight skirt came into being. I had a few bright moments when they were exploiting the flat chest as denoting women with high I.Q.'s, but then someone revealed a certain clearly unflat movie star's 135 (I.Q. that is) and shot *that* theory down.

Here's my basic equipment, if you fashion moguls care to check it out, but frankly it doesn't look too encouraging.

Shoulders: Two of them. Unfortunately they don't match. One hooks up higher than the other, which they tell me is quite common among housewives who carry fat babies, heavy grocery bags, and car chains.

Midriff: If I can't tighten up the muscles in time for beach exposure perhaps I can use it for a snack tray.

Eyes: Some people with myopic vision look sexy. I look like I have myopic vision. Don't tell me what to do with my eyebrows. I tried several things and either look like Milton Berle or Bela Lugosi with a sick headache.

Waist: It's here somewhere. Probably misfiled.

Hips: Here. They weren't built in a day, friend, so don't expect miracles. Right now, they couldn't get a rise out of a factory whistle.

32

Knees: Let me put it this way. A poet at a neighborhood cocktail party once described them as "divining rods that could get water out of the Mojave Desert."

Legs: Ever wonder who got what Phyllis Diller discarded?

Guts: Hardly any.

Tell you what. If I don't "shape up" by June, go on to the beach without me. Stop on the way back and I'll serve you a dish of homemade shortcake, topped with fresh strawberries crusted in powdered sugar and wallowing in a soft mound of freshly whipped cream.

MARCH 5 — MAY 6

i WANT TO bE MORE THAN

just ANOTHER pRETTy FACE ...

TALENT is a big thing.

Most of us can't be like the optimist who was given a barn full of fertilizer and ran through it pell mell shouting, "I know there's a pony here somewhere." We wonder where we were when talent was passed out. Making Jockey shorts for Ken dolls? Fashioning angels out of toilet tissue rolls? Baking no-cal cupcakes for fat Girl Scouts?

Why do we feel so dumb? So out of touch with the world? So lacking in self-confidence? As you look at the reflection in the mirror, your brush rollers towering high above you, your cold sore shimmering from ointment, you mumble to yourself, "I want to be more than just another pretty face. I want to make some difference in this world. Just once I want to stand up at a PTA meeting and say, 'I entertain a motion that we adjourn until we have business more pressing than the cafeteria's surplus of canned tomatoes, and more entertaining than a film on *How Your Gas Company Works for*

You.' " Just once I'd like to have a tall, dark stranger look at me like I wasn't on the sixth day of a five-day deodorant pad. Just once I'd like to have a real fur coat that I could drag behind me on the floor. (Not those 218 hamsters with tranquilizers that I wear to club.)

But me? I couldn't even carry off a trip to Mr. Miriam's Hair Palace. There I stood surrounded by elegance in my simple, peasant headscarf, my wrap-around skirt, my summer tennis shoes, and, my God! *Not Girl Scout socks!*

"Are you a standing?" asked the receptionist.

"A standing what?" I asked.

"Do you have a standing appointment?"

I shook my head.

"I say, you didn't cut your bangs at home with pinking shears or anything, did you?" she asked suspiciously. "Or turn your hair orange with bleach over bleach? Or fall asleep and forget to turn your home permanent off?"

"Oh no," I said. "I just want my hair done because I've been a little depressed since the baby was born."

"Oh," she said softly, "how old is your baby?"

"Twenty-four," I answered.

Because I was unknown to the shop, I drew Miss Lelanie, who had been out of beauty school three days—this time. (The lawsuit with the nasty bald woman is still pending.) With Miss Lelanie, I felt as relaxed as a cat in a roomful of rocking chairs. She didn't say anything, really. She just flipped through my hair like she was tossing a wilted salad. Finally she called in Mr. Miriam to show him what she had found. Both concurred that my ends were split, my scalp diseased, and I was too far over the hill to manufacture a decent supply of hair oil.

"It's all that dry?" I asked incredulously.

"I'd stay away from careless smokers," said Miss Lelanie without smiling.

Miss Lelanie massaged, combed, conditioned, rolled,

brushed, teased, and sprayed for the better part of two hours. Then she whirled me around to look into the mirror. "Why fight it?" I said, pinching the reflection's cheek, "You're a sex symbol." Miss Lelanie closed her eyes as if asking for divine guidance.

I don't mind admitting I felt like a new woman as I walked across the plush carpet, my shoulders squared, my head held high. I could feel every pair of eyes in the room following me.

"Pardon me, honey," said Miss Lelanie, "you're dragging a piece of bathroom tissue on your heel. Want me to throw it away?"

I could have been a standing and I blew it. That's the way it is with me.

Even my own children know I'm a no-talent. There was a time when I could tell them anything and they would believe me. I had all the answers. "Mama, what does the tooth fairy do with all those teeth she collects?" I'd smile wisely and say, "Why she makes them into necklaces and sells them at Tiffany's for a bundle." "What's a bundle, Mama?" "Please, dear," I would say, feigning dizziness, "how much brilliance can Mommy pour into your small head in one day." And so it went. I was their authority on the solar system, the Bible, history, mathematics, languages, fine arts, the St. Lawrence Seaway, air brakes, and turbojets. I even had them believing the traffic lights changed colors when I blew hard and commanded them to "turn green." (So, my kids were a little slow.)

Then one day recently my daughter asked, "Do you know the capital of Mozambique?" "No, but hum a few bars and I'll fake it," I grinned. "Mother," she announced flatly, "you don't know anything!"

That was the beginning. Day by day they chipped away at my veneer of ignorance. I didn't know how to say in French, "Pardon me, sir, but you are standing on my alligator's paw." I didn't know how to find the expanding notation of a number in modern math. (I didn't even know it was missing.) I didn't know the make of the sports car parked across the street, or the exact height of Oscar Robertson. I had never read *Smokey, the Cow Horse.* I didn't even know General Stonewall Jackson always ate standing up so his food would digest better.

In desperation I wrote to Bennington College in Vermont, which, I understood, was offering a course just meant for me.

Sirs:

I read with great interest the possibility of a new course being added to your curriculum, "Boredom of Housewifery." Knowing there will be several million housewives who will invade your city riding trucks, tanks, cars, planes, trains, pogo sticks, rickshaws, bicycles, and skateboards, I hasten to be considered for enrollment.

My background would seem to qualify me. I have three children who are hostile and superior to me mentally, a husband who loves his work and plays the guitar, and a house that depresses me. I cry a lot.

I don't seem to know what to do with my time. I think I waste a lot of it. When I am in the car waiting for the children at school I have taken to writing down the car mileage, multiplying it by my age, subtracting the number of lost mittens behind the seat, and dividing it by my passengers. Whatever number I come up with, is the number of cookies I allow myself before dinner.

I am not stimulated by housework as are other women I know. They are always doing clever things with old nylon hose and egg cartons. Last month I stuck a four-inch nail into the wall above my sink to hold the unpaid bills. When I tried to share my idea with my friends they said I needed to get out more. Sometimes I think the winter has fifteen months in it.

I have also tried joining various organizations, but this does not seem to solve my problem. Last school year I was Sunshine Chairman of the PTA. It seems I spread more sunshine than the treasury was prepared to spread. They dismissed me with a polite note that read, "It is nice to make people happy, but you don't have to tickle them to death."

You stated that the program at Bennington would be designed to aid wives "whose vital intellectual capacity is sapped by what seems to them like endless hours during which they serve as combination caretakers, nurses, policewomen, and kitchen helpers." I like that.

The announcement did not deal specifically with any of the topics to be discussed, but I am hopeful they will cover "Lies and Other Provocative Sayings" for dinner parties, outings, and class reunions. I'd also like a class in "Conversational Hobbies." I passed up the chance to take "Auto Harp Lessons" because I thought I hadn't been driving long enough.

Sincerely,
Desperate

Needless to say the class was filled before they received my application and I continue to feel inadequate and unsure of

41

myself. Why is this? I can see it in my husband's attitude toward me. The other night he took me to dinner. We were having a wonderful time when he remarked, "You can certainly tell the wives from the sweethearts."

I stopped licking the stream of butter dripping down my elbow and replied, "What kind of a crack is that?"

"Just look around you," he said. "See that sweet young thing staring into her young man's eyes? She's single. Now look at the table next to them. That woman has buttered six pieces of bread and is passing them clockwise around the table. Soon she will cut up everyone's meat within a six-table radius and begin collecting swizzle sticks to take home to the kids. She's obviously married. You can always tell. Married women rarely dance. They just sit there and throw appetizers down their throats like the main course just went out of style. Single women go out to 'dine.' Married women go out to 'eat.'"

All the way home, holding the doggy bag filled with tossed salad out the no-draft so it wouldn't drip through on my coat, I thought about what he said. It was true. Women were in a rut. At parties all the women retired to the living room to relive their birth pains and exchange tuna recipes while the men hovered around the kitchen and attacked the big stuff like strikes, racial differences, and wars.

"Why don't you ever talk with us about those things?" I asked.

"What things?"

"Like wars and economics and the UN?"

He grimaced. "Remember the last time at a party I mentioned Taylor was in Vietnam?" (I nodded.) "And you asked if Burton was there with her?" (I nodded.) "That's why."

"That's not fair," I shouted. "You know I'm nothing at parties. I'm just not large on small talk."

"I noticed that," he retorted, "you spring into the first

chair you see like there are magnets in your garters and you never leave it. You just sit there and watch your feet swell."

"It all seems so ridiculous," I snapped. "The other night at that dreary party, one of your friends, whom I shall call Mr. Teeth for want of a better description, said to me, 'I've been looking for you all evening. What have you been reading lately?'"

"What's wrong with that?"

"Nothing. Only he wasn't even looking at me. His head was pivoting like a red light on a police cruiser all the while. I told him I had read 'The Causes and Effects of Diaper Rash' and he said, 'Good show! The critics in the East raved about it.' He hugged me and left."

"What about Larry Blagley. I saw him talking with you."

"You mean 'Mr. Sincere'?"

"I wish you'd stop tagging my friends those goofy names."

"I was enjoying a good, stiff drink when he said, 'Doesn't water pollution bother you at all?' I nearly choked to death. 'Am I drinking it?' I asked. He said, 'Why I have samples in my lab of that stinking, slimy glob of bilge and garbage that looks like so much sticky, clotted, ropey yuuuuuck. It infiltrates your drinking water and mine. If you saw it, it would make your hair stand on end.' 'Just hearing about it isn't doing much for the liver paste that's stuck in my throat either,' I told him."

"The trouble with you," said my husband, "is you're just too cute for words. Coming over and grabbing my sleeve and insisting we leave this deathly dull group!"

"So, I forgot we were the host and hostess. It's a perfectly natural mistake."

"You ought to get out more. Do something to make your day important. Give you something to talk about in the evening."

He had a point. What did I do all day? The only big thing that had happened was I used the wrong aerosol can for my deodorant and I didn't have to worry about clogged-up nasal passages in my armpits for twenty-four hours. No wonder he never talked to me. Out loud I said defensively, "Women would have more confidence if there were more Viktor Syomins in the world!"

"Who is Viktor Syomin?" he asked.

He was paying attention. "Viktor," I explained "is a little-known Russian whose wife was attending Moscow University until one grim day her professor told her, 'In four years you have failed sixteen courses and you don't know anything.' Now any normal American husband would have looked at his wife and said, 'Face it, Luvie, you're a dum dum,' but not Viktor.

"Viktor stomped into the professor's office and demanded, 'You pass my wife or else.' The professor retorted, '*Chepuka*,' which I think means 'And-so's-your-amoeba-brained-wife.' At any rate, Viktor said, 'You have insulted my wife's intelligence,' and broke the professor's nose.

"It's not important that Viktor's assault and battery case comes up in three months," I concluded angrily. "What is important is that he regards his wife as more than a pretty face. He regards her as a mental equal. You hear that? A mental equal! Now, do you want to hear my hilarious story about the aerosol nasal spray I pffted away under my arms or not?"

After a moment's silence, he grinned. "You've got a big mouth."

It's not much of a talent to go on, but I think I just found a pony in my barn.

The Rocky Road to Self-Improvement

AT SOME POINT in her life a woman will go the "self-improvement" route.

This could mean a $3.95 investment in a Bonnie Prudden exercise record, a short course in Conversational Hebrew, Contract Bridge for Blood and Revenge, Mau Mau Flower Arrangements, or a trip back through time to an ivy-covered university.

These courses do what they are supposed to do. They get a woman out of the house, give her a goal or a dream to hang onto, and focus a little attention on herself for a change. It gives her something to contribute to the conversation at dinner. ("You'll never guess who almost fell into the ceramic kiln and made an ashtray of herself!") In short, it gets her out of the proverbial rut.

You take my neighbor Marty. Marty is what we always called a "child-geared" woman. When her pediatrician recommended she use baby talk to communicate with her youngsters, Marty was the first to crawl around on all fours slobbering uncontrollably and gurgling, "No, nee, now, noo, noo."

45

We wondered about it, but Marty said it was a new theory, and she owed it to her kids to try it. That was ten years ago. Today Marty's children talk like Fulbright Scholarship winners. It's Marty who can't kick the baby-talk habit. For example, the other night she said to her husband, "I've laid out your jammies and your bow wow. As soon as you drink your moo cow, you can give Mama a sugar and go upsie-daisy to beddie-bye." Sterling (Marty's husband) just looked at her and said quietly, "I've been thinking, Marty, maybe you oughta have your tongue fixed. I think you're regressing. Have you considered a self-improvement speech course to enlarge your vocabulary?"

Marty was hurt and shocked. She hadn't realized her speaking habits were that bad. Thus was born Marty's "Word a Day" improvement course. It worked very simply. Every morning Marty would get down the large dictionary to her encyclopedia set and flip through it at random. With eyes closed she would point to a word on a page. That was her word for the day. By her own rules she would be compelled to use the word in a sentence at least five times before the sun went down.

We bled for poor Marty. We really did. Her word-for-the-day was sometimes impossible to work into everyday conversation. Like tse-tse fly. At a woman's luncheon Marty threw it out. "Oh, is that a tse-tse fly?" "No," said her hostess coldly, "that is a raisin and I'll thank you to keep your voice down while I am serving it." Or at a cocktail party when she was telling her husband's boss, "I was lying around 'supine' all morning until the mailman came." At his shocked reaction she added quickly, "That's not a dirty word. It's an adjective meaning lying down, lethargic."

Usually it wasn't too tricky to pick out her word-for-the-day by the number of times she used it. We recorded one sentence as follows: "My problems have been infinitesimal lately, but then I say to myself every morning, 'Marty, you

46

are too young to let infinitesimal things bother you. At this rate you'll end up with infinitesimal flu!'" (Three down and two to go.)

As the pressures of home and family increased it became apparent that poor Marty often had no time to look up the meanings of her words. Thus, we would hear her lament, "I have always wanted to play the clavicle." Or, "I never win at Monotony. The kids buy up all the railroads and fertilities and where does that leave me?"

We heard her self-improvement route ended one night when she asked her husband, "Did Fred pass his civil service elimination or was he having one of those days?"

Marty told us her husband said to her, "Martykins, let's find our way back to snookums, horthies, and moo cows. I liked you better when I couldn't understand a word you were saying."

That's one of the hazards of self-improvement. People overdo, and before you know it, they're taking themselves seriously.

We've often said that's what happened to poor Myrtle Flub. Myrtle was a real golf enthusiast. We met her in a six-week golf clinic at the YWCA. To the rest of us, golf was something to do with your hands while you talked. (Unless you smoked. Then, you never had to leave the clubhouse.) With Myrtle it was different. Whenever we got a foursome together, it was always Myrtle who insisted on keeping the scores in ink. Her clubs were never rusted or dulled by wads of bubble gum. (She was horrified the day I found a pair of child's training pants in my golf bag.)

She always played by the book. This was upsetting. We used to try to jazz up the game a bit. For example, if you forgot to say, "Mother, may I?" before you teed off, you had to add a stroke. If you clipped the duck on the pond and made him quack, you didn't have to play the sixteenth hole at all, and if you had more than fifteen strokes on one hole, you didn't have to putt out. This used to drive Myrtle crazy. She never understood why we allowed each other five "I didn't see you swings" in one game.

Then one day she arrived at the course, bubbling with excitement. "I've found a way to take points off my score," she said. (At last, we thought, she's going to cheat like the rest of us.)

"I have just read this article by a British obstetrician who says pregnant women play better golf than women who are not pregnant. He conducted this extensive survey and discovered golf scores were bettered by ten and fifteen strokes."

"But surely," we gasped, "you're not seriously considering . . ."

"If the road to motherhood is paved with birdies, pars, and eagles," she answered, "call me Mom."

The first few months of pregnancy, Myrtle wasn't too sensational on the golf course. She was nauseous. Her normally neat golf bag was a mass of soda cracker crumbs and once when I offered her a piece of cold pizza, she quit playing. Right there on the fifth hole, she quit.

During the early fall, she had a bit of trouble with swollen ankles, so her salt intake and her golf games were kept at a minimum. "Just wait until spring," she said. "I'll be the talk of the club." She was. When Myrtle tried to tee off it was like trying to land on an aircraft carrier without radar. She couldn't see her feet, let alone her ball. To be blunt, she was too pregnant to putt.

Last week we dropped by Myrtle's house en route to the golf course. (She'll resume play when the baby is older.) We talked about the good doctor's survey. "Who is this man?" asked one of the girls. "A medical doctor," Myrtle insisted, "who has done extensive research on women golfers. Here is the picture and the clipping."

We looked in disbelief. There was no doubt in our minds. He was the same man who played behind us the day we dodged the sprinkling system and made the rule that if you got wet, you had to drive the golf cart in reverse back to the clubhouse.

Boy, men sure are bad sports.

I have traveled the self-improvement route on a few occasions myself. A few years back, I found myself not only talking to a fishbowl of turtles, I started to quarrel and disagree with them.

As I told the registrar who was conducting some informal evening classes in the high school, "I want to acquire some skills and the self-confidence to go with them. I don't want to leave this world without some important contribution that will show I've been here. Is the '500 Ways with Hamburger' class filled yet?" It was.

She suggested a class called "Let's Paint." I explained to her I was a beginner. She assured me that "Let's Paint" was a class for amateur artists who had never before held a paintbrush in their hands. She should have added "between their toes or stuck in their ears," because they most certainly wielded them from every other point.

My first table partner was a slim blonde who sprung open her fishing-tackle box and ninety dollars worth of oil paints fell out. She hoisted her canvas on a board like a mast on a sailboat and in twenty minutes had sketched and shaded an impressionistic view of the Grand Canyon in eight shades of purple.

"What are you working on?" she asked, not taking her eyes from her work.

"It's nothing really," I said. "Just a little something I felt like doing today."

She grabbed my sketchbook. "You're tracing a snowman from a Christmas card?"

My next table partner was an elderly woman who confessed she hadn't had a canvas in front of her for years. I'm no fool. She had her own dirty smock and, I suspect, her own scaffold from which she retouched the ceiling of the Sistine Chapel on weekends.

"What have we here?" she bubbled, grabbing my sketch pad. "It's a kitchen window, isn't it? You don't have to label things, my dear. It detracts from the work. Of course, if you don't mind a suggestion, your curtains are a little stiff and stilted. Curtains billow softly."

"Well, ordinarily mine would too," I said, "but I put too much starch in them the last time. You can crack your shins on them."

My next table partner was a young wife awaiting the arrival of her first child. "Did you have any trouble with your still life of the fruit and the pitcher?" she asked shyly.

"Not really," I said, pulling out a sheet of sketch paper with only a few scattered dots on it.

"But the grapes, bananas, and apples?"

"My kids ate them."

"And the pitcher?"

"Dog knocked it off the table."

"And the little dots?"

"Fruit flies."

I like having a table to myself. Talking distracts me from my serious work.

Diseases I'd Tell My Doctor About If It Weren't Wednesday Afternoon

A: ACUTE POSSESSIONITIS. "I've got this problem, Doctor. Lately I've been experiencing a fierce sense of possession. I want to have a closet all my own, a dresser drawer that is all mine and no one else's and personal things that belong only to me. I want to share my life with my family, mind you, but not my roll of scotch tape. Can you understand that?"

50

He smiled. "I think so. Why don't you tell me about it?"

"I guess I first noticed it one night at the dinner table. I took a bite out of this fig newton and set it down. When I went to pick it up again one of the children was popping it into his mouth. 'That's my fig newton,' I said, my lip beginning to quiver. 'You can get another one,' he grinned. 'I don't want another one,' I insisted. 'That was *my* fig newton and you had no right to take it!' He giggled, 'I knew it was your fig newton.' 'Then why did you take it?' I shouted. 'Because I'm nasty and maladjusted,' he shouted back.

"From then on, Doctor, I became terribly conscious of personal items of mine that were being used without my permission. I discovered the family was using my eyebrow pencils to write down messages by the telephone. My Sunday black earrings were the eyes of a snowman. My lace headscarf was the stole of a Barbie doll. My eyebrow tweezers were dissecting a frog. Even my chin strap was filled with buckshot and was on maneuvers in the back yard.

"I can't begin to describe the resentment that began to

build. I finally bought a very large old desk that would house all my personal belongings. It was marvelous. It had forty-five pigeonholes, secret drawers, and sliding panels, and if you didn't hold the lid just right it would fall down and snap your arm off. I transferred all my valuables to the desk like a pack rat anticipating a long winter.

"For a while, things went well. Then things began to slip away from me. My paper clips one by one. My cotton balls. And my rubber bands. (I even disguised them in an old laxative box.) But I'm tired, Doctor. I can't fight anymore."

He smiled. "You're suffering from an old 'return-to-your-single-status' psychosis where you enjoyed some rights and independence. It can happen in an eighteen-year-old marriage. Let me give you a prescription." He stood up, removed the pillow from his chair, unzipped the cover and removed the key. He proceeded to the sixth brick in the fireplace, where he extracted a small box and unlocked it. "My prescription blanks," he laughed nervously. "If I don't hide them from my nurse she uses them for scratch pads."

"I understand," I said.

B: DRAGGING POSTERIER. "Doctor, according to national statistics, I make a dollar fifty-nine an hour. My fringe benefits are few. I get bed and board, a weekly trip to the discount house to listen to the piped-in music, and all the aspirin I can throw down.

"My problem is Sunday work. I am the only one in the house who works on Sundays. It's the same old saw. Everyone pads around all morning in pajamas, running through the comics in their bare feet, and lolling around on the beds like a group of tired Romans waiting for Yvonne deCarlo to appear with a trayful of tropical fruit."

"While you?"

"While I whip around the house getting meals, making beds, finding mates to white gloves, and keeping the fire exits clear of debris."

"And they do nothing?"

"Nothing is right. They eat and watch television. One morning I found them watching test patterns on television. They thought it was a golf show with a diagram pointing out the yardage to the cup."

"What happens when you sit down to relax?"

"One gets a bee caught in his nose. They rub poison oak into their pores. Sometimes they nip away at the paint thinner. Nine out of our last ten emergencies happened on Sunday. Once I almost got a nap. Then my husband said, 'You look bored. Let's clean the garage.'"

"What about the evenings?"

"Evenings are memory time. They remember they need an American flag out of the attic for a school play. One can't take a bath because his toenail is falling off, and somewhere along the line I must give birth to twenty-four pink cupcakes. It's my attitude that bothers me. Last Sunday I did a mean thing, Doctor. I flushed them out of their beds at 7 A.M. yelling, 'You're all going to be late for school.' They staggered around the driveway in the final stages of shock."

"There's no reason for you to have a guilt complex," he explained. "We all have our threshold of endurance. Just put it out of your mind."

"I can't, Doctor. You should hear what I've got planned for next Sunday!"

C: GLUE-BREATH.   "It happened the other morning, Doctor. My cleaning woman approached me and said, 'You may fire me for this, but you've got glue-breath.'

"'But I use a mouthwash,' I insisted. She backed up, weaving unsteadily and said, 'That soda pop isn't doing the job.' In my heart I knew she was right, but I can't help myself. Like most other housewives in America, I succumbed a few years ago to the lure of trading stamps. At first, it was innocent enough. We saved a couple of books and got a croquet

53

set for the kids . . . then a few more books for a lawn trimmer for Dad . . . and finally eight or so books for a leg shaver for me . . . things we really needed.

"Then one day we read a story in the newspaper about a New York zoo that bought a gorilla for 5,400,000 trading stamps. Just reading about all those stamps gave our family a case of redemption fever. We gathered around the dining room table after dinner and began to speculate on what would happen if we upped our consumption of gasoline, oil, tires, windshield wipers, and sunglasses from Bernie's Service Station. 'In three years,' my husband shouted, 'we could buy the New York Mets!'

"Our son figured out if we could get doctors, lawyers, and the sanitary department to issue trading stamps we might even amass enough to earn a Rhino hunt weekend for two in scenic Kenya. We went half crazed with desire. One of the children vowed to start saving for Rhode Island, another for Richard Nixon's older daughter . . . another for a do-it-yourself missile site for the back yard. I personally wanted to visit the Senior Citizen Center to which Cary Grant belonged. The possibilities were crazy and without limits.

"From that day on, our entire buying habits changed. We often ran out of gas looking for a station with our brand of stamps. We bought food we hated to get bonus stamps. In desperation, we even switched to a newly-formed church across town that gave one hundred and twenty trading stamps each time we attended. (We now worship a brown and white chicken with a sunburst on its chest.)

"I know it sounds ridiculous, but I have pasted stamps in 1563 books. I'll match that against J. Paul Getty's stamp books any day of the week! Someone in the family guards them twenty-four hours a day and we count them once a week. We stage mock fire drills from time to time so we can evacuate them quickly in case of fire. In the event of a nuclear attack, we have instructions to empty out the drink-

ing water and save the stamp books. Trading stamps have possessed me, Doctor. What do you think?"

The doctor tapped his pencil slowly on the desk. "I personally think you are some kind of a nut with fuzzy breath, that's what I think. What in the world are you going to buy with 1563 books?"

"When I fill five more pages, Doctor," I said stiffly, "I will own this office building. And if I were you, I wouldn't have any more magazines sent to this address!"

D: CAR POOL ALLERGY. "You see, Doctor, children see their mothers as symbols of some kind—hot apple pie, delicate perfume, a soft kiss to heal a scraped knee.

"My children see me as four wheels, a motor, and a drive shaft. I am Snow White with a set of car keys. Peter Pan off in a cloud of blue exhaust. Mary Poppins with fifteen gasoline credit cards.

"People are always talking about men who commute. I don't feel sorry for them. At least they drive on designated roads where their only annoyances are a few bad drivers and a few dozen police cars camouflaged as spirea bushes.

"But women in car pools! Women get cuffed with lunch boxes while they're driving. Women have to cut bubble gum out of their hair with scissors. Women have to charter new routes over barren fields and swamplands looking for the 'Blue team on Diamond 12.'

"Frankly, Doctor, I've been involved in so many car pools I'm beginning to walk like Groucho Marx. This business of chauffeuring really began to bother me about two weeks ago. I pulled up in front of a traffic light and five girls piled in. One said, 'Carol, tell your mother to turn right at the next street.' A girl called Carol said, 'She's not my mother. I thought she was your mother.' 'No,' said the other voice, 'My mother wears glasses. Or is it my father who wears glasses? Hey, gang, is this anyone's mother?'

" 'The back of the head does look familiar,' said one. 'Did you take a group of girls on school patrol on a tour of bus station restrooms recently?' I shook my head no.

" 'I got it,' said another. 'You brought the garbage home from Girl Scout Camp! I remember now. It was out-of-season so we couldn't bury it. When she came to pick up her group she got stuck with bringing the garbage home. Sorry, but I didn't recognize you without all those fruit flies.'

"I nodded affirmatively. How long ago was it when I begged for wheels of my own? A car was going to restore independence to my dreary life, open up lines of communication to a whole new world of culture and entertainment. It was going to free me from the bonds of my daily routine. What happened?

"When I left the girls off, I ended up with two small passengers, my Wednesday afternoon kindergarten drop-offs. 'I'm five years old,' one of them announced to the other. 'I wonder how old she is.' (Note: Small children always refer to the driver in the third person, never directly. This destroys the impersonal driver-passenger relationship.) 'I'm eight years old!' I yelled back impulsively.

"'Do you think she's really eight years old?' asked the other one.

"'I'm big for my age,' I added.

"'My mother is that big and she's thirty-two,' said the first one.

"'Big people act funny sometimes,' said the second child.

"'Yeah,' said the first child, 'but it beats walkin'.'"

E: IDENTITY PAINS. "I might as well confess it before you hear it from someone else, Doctor. I've found my identity.

"You can't imagine what this means. People who have considered me a friend for years shout, 'Fraud, fake, and traitor.' Some of them have burned copies of *Hints from Heloise* on my front yard. I know I will be asked to turn in my Betty Friedan signet ring. Nevertheless it is true.

"I wasn't real took with the movement for women's equality in the first place. What with carrying out the trash, changing fuses, cutting the grass, and fertilizing the shrubbery, any more equality would kill me. You have to know I'm the type if Carrie Nation had called and said, 'Would you like to make a contribution to your sex?' I'd probably have said, 'My husband gives at the office.'

"I don't know. I tried to have a real mystique going for me, but I didn't get too much mileage out of it. I used to shuffle through the house saying, 'Who am I? Where am I? Where am I going?' All I did was scare the Avon lady half to death. I even said to my husband one night, 'You know, I think I've lost my identity,' and without looking up he said, 'It's probably with your car keys . . . wherever they are.'

"When I told my mother about my 'Oedipus conflict and sibling rivalry that had embedded themselves into my personality,' she said, 'What kind of language is that for a mother?'

"Well, the first clue to my identity came one day when the phone rang and someone said, 'Hello, Erma.' I tell you my eyes misted up like Ben Cartwright on *Bonanza* when his

57

horse goes lame. 'What did you call me?' I asked slowly. The voice repeated the name. That was it. That must be my identity. Feverishly I went through my billfold in my purse and emptied out a stack of credit cards, a YWCA membership, a library card, and a driver's license. They all bore the same name.

"I raced to the bedroom and began rummaging through drawers. There were old report cards signed by me, monogrammed handkerchiefs, and autographed copies of books scrawled, 'To Erma.' At last I knew my real identity.

"Then a card fell to the floor. It was addressed to Mrs. Erma Bombeck, Girl Scout cookie captain. My first real breakthrough. I not only knew who I was but what I was. *I was a commissioned officer in the cookie corps!*

"I felt wonderful and proud, Doctor. My mystique had been solved. My problem now is I can't remember where I put the cookies.'"

Parting with Money Is Taxing

THERE WERE REALLY ONLY two men I knew who ever got a laugh out of paying their income taxes. One was cheating the government and getting away with it. The other had a sick sense of humor and would probably have set up a concession stand at the Boston Tea Party and sold sugar cubes and lemon slices.

Sitting up with a sick taxpayer is no picnic. At best "How to live with your husband until his W-2 forms are filed" is pure agony. I have done it for years and these are the lessons I've reaped:

1. Never try to talk your husband out of his depression over his taxes. The last woman I heard who stood at her husband's elbow waving a flag and chanting, "Be thankful for

Mom and apple pie," is now living with her mother and working in a bakery. This is no time to fool around.

2. Never suggest that he file his tax return early. There is nothing that will unsettle a man more than being jammed in a post office with a group of New Year's revelers who are filing early only because they are getting a refund. Better to have him in the cortege of cars that slowly inch their way to the mailbox at midnight of the April deadline, while a sullen group on the post office steps chants, "We shall overcome."

3. Keep the children out of his path. From January through April they cease to have names. They become Deduction A, Deduction B, and Deduction C. Mentally he begins to add up what he has invested in their teeth, arches, sports program, fine arts, education, clothes, food, lodging, entertainment, vitamins, and social welfare. Once he has figured out that $600 wouldn't keep them in catsup and breakfast cereal, his resentment reaches a danger point.

4. Anticipate his low days. When he is virtually drowning in a sea of canceled checks, receipts, memos, and statements of interest and income, offer enthusiastically to have your gall bladder taken out next year to increase his medical deduction. Promise to adopt an orphan Parisian chorus girl, make a large donation to the indigent at the Polo Club, invest unwisely, lose heavily at Chinese checkers, buy an office building on credit.

Above all, be ready to produce explanations or at least to discuss any expenditure from a cold capsule to a major purchase like swimming lessons for your daughter.

"How in the name of all that is sane did you spend $175 for swimming lessons?" he shouted, the veins standing erect in his neck. "I could have gotten Flipper to tutor her in our own bathtub for $50."

"Actually the swimming lessons were only $4 for ten weeks at the 'Y,' but I encountered some extras."

"What extras?"

59

"Extras! There was 49 cents for a nose plug."

"That leaves $170.51."

"And the parking. I think that amounted to $35."

"$35?"

"I parked in a towaway zone. Then one night we stayed downtown and had dinner and went to a movie. That amounted to about $10."

"That narrows it down to $125.51."

"Of course, $12 or so went for bribes."

"Another towaway zone?"

"No, to keep our boys from playing with the paper towels in the restroom and skating on the lobby floors. I had to bribe them with food and things. After all, my pride is worth something."

"That's 'Pride: $12,'" he mused.

"Yes and don't forget the bedspreads. I get to town so rarely I felt I had to run over and look at the bedspreads on sale. I bought two. Take away $24.73."

"That leaves $88.78."

"Well, about $15 went for medication when she forgot to

dry her hair and caught cold. If you're concerned about the waste of pills, I could pack them in her lunch."

"Don't be cute," he said. "What happened to the other $73.78?"

"My goodness, there were a lot of things. Name tapes for the towels, new swimming bag, new headlight for the mail truck I hit, and don't forget the nose plug."

"That was 49 cents, wasn't it?" he asked, unconsciously moistening his ballpoint pen on his tongue.

Laugh at income tax? My dear, I would sooner put out my foot and trip Tiny Tim.

Sick . . . Sick . . . Sick . . .

HER STORY:

Actually I was looking forward to Leonard's being home, even if he was recuperating from minor surgery. We were going to have leisure breakfasts, giddy coffee breaks, pore over old picture albums and maybe even harmonize on a few reckless choruses of "Mexicali Rose."

I don't know what went wrong. I ran trays like I was working the dark corner of a drive-in. I fluffed pillows, rubbed his back, delivered papers, smoothed sheets, and was summoned from every room in the house. Of course, Leonard was never able to stand pain. When he suffered a paper cut in '59, I never left his bedside. The doctor said it was my strength that pulled him through.

"Did I tell you I was awake during the entire operation?" he yelled down the hallway.

"Yes!"

"Did I tell you about that herd of vampires who drew blood from me every hour of the day and night?"

"Yes!"

By the second week he had me looking up phone numbers

of all his old Army buddies at Ft. Dix, digging out the ouija board, finding out how much insurance he had on his car (among other research projects), and nursing his pothus plant back to life. ("All right then, *you* tell Miss Cartwright her gift pothus died because it was pot-bound. Go ahead! Break an old woman's heart!")

"You hear me out there?" he'd shout. "While you're flitting around the countryside, stop off at the library and get us a book on playwriting. You hear? We could write a hit play together, you and I."

By the third week he was approaching full strength. He toured the house and discovered the kitchen cupboards were ill-planned, something strange had died in the utility room, and what this family really needed was a well-organized, well-planned duty roster.

His final week was probably his finest hour. He was in his "communications" syndrome, or as we called it, "Chopping Off at the Mouth."

"You tell Ed at the garage I said if he doesn't set that motor up he can jolly well push it all the way to Detroit with the broken nose I am going to give him when I get out of this bed. Got that? As for Clark at the office, you just tell him for me that I've dealt with his kind before and if he thinks he can pull this off while I am flat on my back he's got another thought coming. Remind him what happened in '48."

"What happened in '48?" I asked intently.

"Nothing, but Clark won't remember either. And another thing. You collar that grass cutter you hired and tell him for me to set that mower back where I had it. I don't want a putting green, just some front yard grass left."

I guess I know why the Good Lord had women bear the children. Men would have delegated the job!

HIS STORY:

Actually I was looking forward to staying home with Doris to help her over her bout with the flu. If a man can't pitch

62

in and manage his own kids and his own house, I always say, what's he good for?

I don't know what went wrong. Lord knows I was doing the best I could under the circumstances. I tried to bring a little order to her kitchen, but when I flung open the cabinet doors and read the headlines on the shelf paper, DEWEY CONCEDES TO TRUMAN, I knew I was in for it. I lined up the kids and put them to work. Doris lets them get away with too much.

"Why in heaven's name does your mother keep the marshmallows in the oven?" I asked.

"She hides them," they said.

"Now you kids hike this turkey roaster up to the attic. She only uses it on state occasions. Give me those cocktail onions so I can put them on a lower shelf where they'll be within easy reach. Now, where's the coffee?"

"In the stove drawer, Daddy."

"What's wrong with keeping it in the canister marked C-O-F-F-E-E?"

"Because she hides the P-O-P-C-O-R-N there."

We were doing just fine, mind you, when she yells from the bedroom, "Why don't all of you go out and rotate the tires on the car or make lamps out of old bowling pins or something?" That's gratitude for you. Doris is a bit of Mama's girl. Faints when she has to remove a corn pad. I don't like to criticize her while she's flat on her back, but there was stuff in her refrigerator so old that a casserole actually attacked me and drew blood. "If you don't keep those left-overs moving," I warned her, "you're going to have to open a pharmaceutical house."

"Who was on the phone?" she yelled.

"Just the principal. Don't worry."

"What did he want?" she persisted.

"Nothing. He was just explaining the school's policy on bedroom slippers."

63

She groaned. "Why are the kids wearing bedroom slippers?"

"Because we can't find their shoes. They're probably on the washer, but we can't get to the washer until after seven. I figure the water from the washer should crest at that hour and then begin to recede."

"You mean the washer overflowed?"

How's that for innocence. If I've told her once, I've told her fifty times to put the little socks and underwear in a bag and then the pump wouldn't get stopped up, but she never listens. I didn't get so much as a "Thank you" for going door to door collecting for her "Research for Sweating Feet" drive, or for driving fifteen Cub Scouts on a tour of a frozen food locker.

If Doris only ran a home like men ran their offices, I wouldn't have to take up so much time in organization. All I did was slip a little note on her night stand asking her to fill in her reply on the following:

1. How do you turn on the garbage disposal?

2. How do you turn off the milkman?

3. How do you remove a Confederate flag tattooed in ink on the forehead of a small boy?

4. Where is the anise for the chili?

5. What is your mother's phone number?

That was certainly no reason for her to groan and start getting dressed. Sometimes I wonder why the Good Lord gave the job of having children to women, when men could organize the process and turn them out in triplicate in half the time.

MAY 7 — july 9

how do you GET OUT of
this chicken outfit?

"PARDON ME," said the milkman politely tipping his hat, "but I think you put the wrong note in the bottle this morning. This one reads, 'HELP! I'm being held a prisoner by an idiot with a set of wrenches in a house that has been without running water for three days. How do you get out of this chicken outfit?'"

"You're new on the route, aren't you?" I asked.

"Yes, ma'am," he said, his eyes looking for an escape hatch through the taxus. "This sounds like a call for help," he hesitated. "I just take these bottles back to the plant to be sterilized and filled with milk again. I don't drop them in Lake Erie or anything."

"I know that!" I said irritably. "It's just that I'm married to this home-improvement drop-out and every once in a while I just have to try something!"

He didn't understand about modern marriages. I could tell that by the way he bolted to the truck. Some marriages are made in heaven with stardust in the eyes. Others are made in haste with piles of sawdust whipping around the feet.

Mine was the latter, which I discovered less than two weeks after I was married. My husband came home from the drugstore ecstatic with two cigar boxes under his arm. He rushed to the basement, nailed them together, painted them dark green and called them "shadow boxes."

Despite the fact they looked like two cigar boxes nailed together with "King Edward" bleeding through, I avowed they belonged in the Metropolitan. While showing guests through the apartment I would chin myself on them to prove their strength and exclaim that if I had known what a clever dog he was I would have married him in his playpen.

As usual, I overacted.

How was I to know that later he would saw an opening in our back door to let the dog *in*, then consider how to keep the snow *out*? How could I suspect that he would enclose our garbage cans with a fence so high you had to catapult the garbage and hope for the best? How could I imagine his fifth-grade practical arts course would become a way of life?

For a while he went through his built-in period. Everything in the house had to be contained, stacked, attached, enclosed and out of sight. The garage had shelf units to the ceiling that held all the dried-up cans of paint, old coffee cans, and discarded license plates. He enclosed the television set, the bookcases, the stereo, washer, dryer, bar, clothes, blankets, linens, sewing machine, and cleaning supplies. I climbed out of bed one morning and proceeded to stretch my arms and yawn. Before I could get my arms to my sides, I was supporting five shelves of cookbooks and a collection of glass elephants.

Later I was to discover he never went to bed on a finished project. Fired with enthusiasm over a plan for improvement, he would spread the room with wall-to-wall ladders, open a myriad of paint cans (ready for spilling), and roll up the draperies into a ball on the sofa. Then he would smile, climb into his coat, and say, "I am off to study the blister beetle in South America. Don't touch a thing until I get back."

On other occasions, he was not as inventive. He'd simply pull the stove out from the wall, remove the oven door, put the bathroom hardware to soak in a kitchen sink full of vinegar, then announce, "I don't have tools like the rest of the fellas. I do the best I can with a Boy Scout ax and crude tools I've been able to fashion out of boulders and buffalo hide. But when you don't have the right tool for the right job, you can't turn out the work of a craftsman."

Eventually the news that I was supporting a home-improvement drop-out was no secret. We were the couple with the screens in all winter and the storm windows in all summer.

We spread grass seed in the snow and put up our TV antennae in an electrical storm.

Even the simple jobs, he attacked with all the grace of a herd of buffalo under fire.

"I was wondering if you could reach behind the washer and put that simple plug into that simple outlet?" I inquired one evening.

"Let's see now," he said surveying the situation. "First, I'll need my Home Workshop Encyclopedia, Volume VIII. Dig that out for me, will you? Get the chapter on 'Outlets: Electrical.' Now, get my utility belt, my insulated gloves, and hard safety hat with the light attachment. They make these utility rooms for pygmies, you know. And with a running jump I'll hoist myself to the top of the washing machine where I'll—"

"Break the washer cycle dial with your big foot," I said dryly. "Look, maybe I'd better do it," I said. "I'm smaller than you and I can just reach over and—"

"This is man's work," he said firmly. "You go finish shoveling the snow off your driveway and leave me to my job at hand."

"No, I'll just stick around in case your eyeballs flash for help."

He lowered himself behind the appliance and inserted the plug—halfway—blowing out all the power on the kitchen circuit. Shocked (but literally), he backed into the dryer vent, disconnecting it. Simultaneously he dropped his flashlight from his helmet into an opening between the walls. For his "big finish" he rapped his head on the utility shelf and opened a hissing valve on the hot water heater with his belt buckle.

I folded my hands and closed my eyes in prayer. "May he never retire."

Ironically, most women envy me my do-it-yourself husband. "At least he does *something!*" said our new neighbor. "You should be thankful for that."

I smiled. "Would you mind sitting in this chair? I wouldn't ask you to move but my husband's leg is coming through the living room ceiling and I wouldn't want him to fall in your lap. Basically he's shy."

She looked rather alarmed as he yelled down through the opening, "Erma! Put an X on what's left of the ceiling so the next time I'll know there's no stud here!"

"I still think it's wonderful," the neighbor persisted, "how you two tackle all kinds of home projects together. I see you out there cutting grass while he trims the hedge and washing the car while he's cleaning out the glove compartment. It's just wonderful."

I was silent a moment, then I pulled my chair closer. "Let me tell you a secret. I have always resented the helpless female. I resent her because I am secretly jealous of her ability to train grown men to 'heel' and sick and tired of having her feel my flexed muscles at parties.

"If I had it to do all over again, I would be one of those helpless females who faints at the sight of antifreeze. But I was the big mouth who, early in marriage, watched my husband try to start the power mower and said, 'If you are trying to start that power mower, Duckey, you had better attach the spark plug, open the gas line so you can get fuel to the distributor, and pull the choke all the way over. Also, if you don't stand on the other side of the mower, you'd better lean against that tree for balance because you are going to lose your right foot.'"

"How masterful," she said, dabbing her forehead with a lace handkerchief.

"Not so masterful," I said. "From that day forward I was awarded custody of the mower. I also had to repair spoutings, clean out the dryer vent, repair the clothesline, build the rock garden, drain and store the antifreeze, and wash the car."

"My goodness," she whispered, "I'm so addle-brained

about cars I scarcely know how to turn on those little globes in the front . . . the . . ."

"Lights," I prompted. "Incidentally, what's that pet name your husband calls you?"

"You mean, 'Satin Pussy Cat'?"

"That's the one. My husband calls me 'Army,' after a pack mule he had in Korea. You're the one who's got it made. I'll bet you never fertilized a lawn, changed a fuse, plunged a sink, hosed out a garbage can, or hung curtain brackets."

She threw back her head, revealing her slim, white throat, and laughed. "Why I get lightheaded whenever I step up on a curb."

"Take today. I've got this clogged-up washer. I can either ring for Rube Goldberg and his wonder-wrenches, or I can try to fix the thing myself."

She smiled slyly. "I'll bet it's your turbo pump that's clogged. All you have to do is remove the back panel, take out the pulsator, disconnect the thermoschnook, and use a spreckentube to force out the glunk. Then put on a new cyclocylinder, using a No. four pneusonic wrench, and you're back in the laundry business."

"Why you helpless little broad—er fraud! You could run General Motors from a phone booth. You're faking it, aren't you? That helpless routine is all show. And what does it get you? Nothing but dinner rings, vacations out of season, small fur jackets, and a husband standing breathless at your elbow. Do you know the last time my husband stood breathless at my elbow I had a chicken bone caught in my throat? Is it too late for me? Do you suppose a woman over thirty-five could learn to be helpless?"

She smiled. "Of course. And you can start by asking that nice milkman if he'd be a dear and drop your note in the bottle into Lake Erie, if it isn't too much trouble . . ."

The Outdoor Nut

I HAVE ALWAYS BEEN led to believe a good marriage was based on things a couple had in common.

A while back I read where Liz Taylor, commenting on one of her earlier marriages, said the common bond between her and her husband was that they wore the same sweater size. The obvious conclusion must be: They just don't make sweaters anymore like they used to. In reality, it's what you *don't* have in common that holds a marriage together.

Early in my marriage (my honeymoon, to be exact) I discovered I was married to an outdoor nut. As I sat there in a cabin on Rainbow Trout Lake fingering my nosegay, I said, "What do you want? Me? Or a great northern pike?" Friends have since told me I would have fared better in the competition had I picked a smaller fish. I was pushing.

Through the years the condition has only worsened. All

73

winter long my husband has what is commonly referred to in fishing circles as the fever. He sharpens his hooks, teases the feathers on his lures, reads articles on "Backlash Lake" and "Angler's Paradise," and follows me around the kitchen inviting me to watch his wrist action.

His wading boots (boots that extend up to the armpits so that when the water pours in, you are assured of drowning instantly) hang on a hook in the garage with all the readiness of a fireman's hat. Whenever a fellow fisherman gives the hysterical cry "The white bass are running!" he grabs his boots and does the same.

Actually I have never known the white bass to do anything else but run. They certainly never stop long enough to nibble at the bait. Theoretically the bass are always on a "hot lake." Now a "hot lake," I discovered, is where all the "hot liars" hang out. The reasons they give for the fish not biting are enough to stagger the imagination.

1. The fish aren't biting because the water is too cold.
2. The water is too hot.
3. The fish are too deep.
4. It is too early.
5. It is too late.
6. They haven't stocked it yet.
7. They're up the river spawning.
8. The water skiers and motorboats have them stirred up.
9. They've been poisoned by pollution.
10. They just lowered the lake level.
11. They're only biting on bubble gum and bent nails.
12. Some novice has just dumped his bait into the water and they're stuffed to the gills and can't eat another bite.
13. They haven't been biting since the Democrats have been in power.

When outdoor camping became the symbol of togetherness, I knew my husband wouldn't rest until he had me reeking of insect repellent and zipped into a sleeping bag out where the deer and the antelope play.

I've relived that first camping trip in my mind a thousand times. (They tell me only shock treatments could erase it permanently.) I've tried to analyze why we failed. First, I think we had seen too many Walt Disney films and expected more help from the animals than we got. Second, unlike other families, our family does not have the necessary primitive instincts for survival. We are lucky to get the car windows rolled down to keep from suffocating.

I personally opposed erecting our tent in a driving rain. I thought it would put us all in a bad humor. As it was, no sooner had we driven the last peg when a passerby remarked to his companion, "Look at that, Lucille. It's listing worse than the *Titanic* just before she went down." Then my husband poked his head out of the flap and retaliated, "Same to you, fella," and I don't mind telling you it took two stanzas of "Nearer My God to Thee" to quiet them down. From that moment on, the bathhouse set referred to us as "Old Crazy Tent."

The rain presented a bit of a problem—all fifteen days of it. This took a lot of ingenuity. "I don't like to mention it," I said one afternoon, "but I think this weather and this tent are beginning to get on my nerves."

"Why do you say that?" asked my husband.

"Because I spent an entire morning counting the grains of sand in the butter."

"The kids keep busy enough," he said.

He was right. They examined their hair follicles under a flashlight, clipped toenails, ate crackers in someone else's sleeping bag, took the labels off the canned goods, kept a rather complete log of frequent visitors to the bathhouse, and wrote postcards home telling everyone what a "blast" they were having.

On the sixteenth day good fortune struck. A hysterical

woman from the next tent heard via her transistor that we were in for a tornado. I combed my hair and put on a trace of lipstick. It was the first time I'd been out of the tent in two weeks.

Sitting in the car, with the thorny feet of one of the kids in my ribs, I heard someone from the back seat say, "We'll survive all right." He had thought to grab two cans without labels on his way out. One was a small tin of cocktail weiners, the other was a can of cleanser.

On the eighteenth day it became apparent we had three choices to make: (a) Fix the tent so we could stand up in it, (b) Have our legs fixed so they would measure no more than one-fourth the length of our bodies, (c) Get into the car and make a side trip.

The children voted for a visit to a deer farm about twenty miles from the campsite. It was one of those commercial little ventures where you pay a price and enter the compound and the deer are roaming free among the visitors. There's also a souvenir shop that sells mother-of-pearl ashtrays, a rocking plane ride that costs a dime and makes the kids throw up, and a popcorn stand. We each bought a box of popcorn and set out to spend a quiet afternoon among these gentle animals with the large trusting eyes.

When I first felt a sharp pinch on my backside, I whispered to my husband, "You devil you." The second time it happened I became quite irritated and turned sharply to face a pair of large, brown trusting eyes and two hoofs on my coat lapels. It seemed popcorn drove the deer half out of their skulls with mad desire. The entire herd charged us, pushing, shoving, nipping. They had one child cornered, another one sobbing in the dirt, and my husband pirouetting on his toes like a ballet dancer. We agreed the tent wasn't much, but it was safe from a deer stampede.

The end of three weeks of camping found all of us "adjusting." Slapping the laundry against a flat rock, walking around with sand in our underwear, and taking a bath in a one-quart saucepan had become a way of life.

Sometimes at night when the campfire glowed and you sipped your coffee in the stillness of the night, you felt you might be present at the creation. The kids intent on listening to animals rustling in the bushes and watching the flickering patterns in the fire forgot to argue with one another. No telephones. No Avon ladies. No television. No lawn mowers. No committee meetings. No vacuum sweepers. Just peace.

Then one night, there was peace no more. A twenty-two-foot trailer slithered into the clearing next to us. We could hear their voices crack through the silence of the lazy morning.

"I swear, Clifford, I don't mind roughing it, but with no electricity to hook up to, this is ridiculous. What am I supposed to do about my electric coffee pot and my blanket and my heater?"

"Don't tell me your problems," he shouted. "What about my shaver and my electric martini stirrer."

"Well, I hope they have a laundromat and a shower house with hot water . . ."

"And a boat dock," he added, "and a swimming pool for the kids. They'll be sick if there's no swimming pool. You know how cold the lakes are."

"Did you check on whether or not they picked up the garbage every day? I don't want a lot of animals around the trailer. I didn't come out here in the wilderness to fight off animals. What in the world is that infernal noise?"

"I think we're near the beach. That water lapping and rolling in all night long is going to drive me crazy. Did you bring my pills, Arlene?"

"Of course, dear. Why don't you set up your screened cabana and listen to the radio? I'll try to rustle you up a drink. I don't suppose that little shopkeeper who looks like Gabby Hayes has ever heard of ice cubes before."

I turned to my husband. "Let's knock the other prop out from under our tent tomorrow and head up toward Blue Water Cove. I hear it's a 'hot lake' and 'the bass are running' like dishonest congressmen."

He grinned. "I think you've got 'the fever.'"

It's summertime and once again our daughter, the Midwest's answer to Tokyo Rose, has been circulating daily bulletins of our vacation plans.

I had one phone call from a woman two blocks over to look up her sister in San Juan, a request from a retired couple for a bushel of grapefruit from Orlando, and just yesterday a carry-out boy winked and said, "Are you really going to Berkeley to burn your library card?"

Actually I'm an advocate of separate vacations: the children's and ours. Or as comedienne Joan Rivers said, "They hated the children and would have separated years ago, but they're staying together for the sake of each other."

There is something about packing five people into a car with nothing to do but tolerate each other that leads to roughhousing, name-calling, eye-gouging, and eventually recoiling next to the spare tire in the trunk. Each individual pursues his or her own antagonistic topic.

The children, for example, will ramble on for miles about the last restroom they visited, describing in intricate details the messages written in lipstick on the walls. Then they will amuse themselves by the hour playing "auto roulette." This is a precarious game of trampling, jostling, and hurling of bodies to see which one gets a seat nearest the window.

Despite the enthusiastic reports from parents that their children broke out in hives from the excitement of viewing the Grand Canyon, we have noted ours couldn't care less. Their interests run toward amusement parks, souvenir shops, miniature golf ranges, zoos with souvenir shops, parks with swings and slides, restaurants with souvenir shops, pony rides, and national monuments with souvenir shops. I get the feeling if we drove the car to Lincoln's Memorial, climbed his leg and spread out a picnic lunch on his lap, one of the kids would observe, "Keep your eyes open for a motel with a heated swimming pool and a nearby souvenir shop."

The compulsive desire to buy a carful of souvenirs before we got to the city limits became so bad, we had to set down some explicit rules for souvenir buying:

Know your history. Don't be lured into buying a genuine replica of a ballpoint pen used by Stephen Foster when he wrote, "I Dream of Jeanie with the Light Brown Hair." (We paid a few dollars more and bought the typewriter used by Thomas Jefferson when he wrote the Declaration of Independence.)

Learn to be crafty. Beware of Indians selling electric blankets, authentic Japanese kimonas made in West Virginia, and President and First Lady T-shirts. (The barbecue sauce we bought, but T-shirts!)

Select a souvenir that will remind you of your visit. This is especially difficult with children who insist on buying a

79

sweat shirt that proclaims, "I'M AN ALCOHOLIC. IN CASE OF EMERGENCY, BUY ME A BEER," from scenic Bar Harbor.

Don't pay exorbitant prices for souvenir items you can buy at home. Take that small Frankenstein toy we bought in Tennessee—the one where you pull a switch and his pants fall down and his face turns red—$3.95, batteries not included. With what I would have saved buying it out of a catalogue, I could have bought that beautiful satin pillow in the Smokies that read, "There's No Salt Like a Mother's Tears."

Lastly, consider how good a traveler your souvenir will be. Once when we bought a bushel of peaches from Georgia, we had to drive steadily with no stops for forty-eight hours to avoid being eaten alive by fruit flies.

On another occasion, all five of us had to ride together in the front seat to avoid conflict of interest with a small alligator in the back seat.

Next to children on a trip, there is nothing more trying than their father. He doesn't go on a trip to enjoy the scenery and relax. He's on a virtual test run to prove his car's performance in a grinding show of speed and endurance equaled only on the salt flats testing grounds.

First, there's the graphic charts he insists be kept listing the mileage, gasoline and oil consumption, and itemized expenses encountered during the trip. Three things usually happen to these charts: (a) They are used to wrap up a half-eaten Popcicle and discarded along the way, (b) They are grabbed in an emergency to squash bugs on the windshield, (c) They are committed to memory and used as a mild sedation on neighbors and friends upon your return.

Next, he will insist you read and interpret road maps. To do this you must consider that you are dealing primarily with a maniac, a driver who wants to arrive at his destination three hours before he leaves home. He abhors heavy traffic, detours, toll stations, construction, and large cities with a population of fifty or more. He is depending upon you to anticipate these discomforts and avoid them at all costs. In short, he is hostile. You will find your road map, folded incorrectly in the glove compartment. Usually it will be a little out of date (listing only the original thirteen colonies). Once when I told my husband we measured but a hairpin and a mint away from our destination, he beat his head on the steering wheel and openly accused me of moving the Mississippi River over two states.

Another challenge is getting the driver of the car to stop for food. Rationalizing that even at the "500," they have pit stops, our driver invariably feeds us on promises of what lies ahead at Futility City.

With bloated stomachs and sharp teeth from gnawing on our safety belts we hit Futility City only to discover one filling station, a hound dog in the middle of the road, and a brightly lighted stand where they sell shaved-ice cones. The hound dog looks interesting.

Since this is to be an honest account of the behavior patterns of the average vacationer, I can't leave out "Mother." Mother climbs into the car and, like an evangelist who just had the tent collapse on her flock, can't resist a captive audience. She goes the discipline route.

I have been known to go across an entire state, ignoring national monuments, freaks of nature, postcard countrysides, faces carved in mountains and herds of wild buffalo, while my long-playing mouth recites misdemeanors the kids made when they were on Pablum. My sermon on "All right now, which one of you clowns turned on the car heater?" extended over three states.

Sometimes mothers are permitted to drive, but only under the following conditions: (1) city traffic at 5 P.M. when the population is 250,000 or over, (2) unmarked dirt roads at midnight, (3) highways under construction with detour signs that have blown over, (4) in a tornado on an eight-lane high-way where the minimum speed is 65 mph.

The irony of all this is that we don't know what a madcap time we're having until we see our vacation on our home movies. In the flickers, we hide our heads in our armpits, dance a jig, act like we're fighting Dempsey for the title, and pull down limbs of trees and point to them like we've just discovered a cure for arthritis.

We've got some wonderful footage on my husband where he is standing on his head removing a fishhook from his underside and mouthing obscenities into the camera. All the rest of us are holding our sides laughing fit to die. There's another classic where my Wallie the Whale waterwings spring a leak and I disappear beneath some lily pads and never surface again. Oh, and there's a thrilling shot of one of the kids being sick on a small fishing boat off the coast of Florida and we are hovering over him offering him salami and may-onnaise sandwiches. That one really breaks us up.

Another vacation this year? You bet. We're firm believers that at least once a year a family ought to get away from it all so they can appreciate good food, plush lodgings, conven-ient stores, and breathtaking scenery—upon their return home after two grim weeks of togetherness.

Must try to remember to send in the boys' camp appli-cations early. You see, I *do* remember last year's disappoint-ment:

Mr. Grim Gruber, Director
Camp Discouragement for Boys
City
Dear Mr. Gruber:

The afternoon mail brought me your fine brochure on Camp Discouragement for Boys. You may or may not re-member me. My son attended your camp last summer for two weeks. (He was the blond boy whose soiled socks stuck to the light bulb in the mess hall.)

We were so pleased with the peace and tranquility we enjoyed in his absence, Mr. Bombeck suggested I rush down before Thanksgiving to make sure you have enrollment space. (He also wanted me to remind you he fought for your freedom in World War II, but I don't like to bring pressure.)

Your camp originally came to our attention as it was the only one we could spell. The previous summer we sent him to Camp Mini-something-or-other and discovered we were obviously misspelling the name of the camp. We kept getting letters from a chieftain in the Blackfoot reservation in North Dakota who thanked us profusely for the cookies and clean socks.

I do hope your fine counselor, Mr. Bley, is well enough to return this summer. I was surprised to hear of his "health problem" as he looked so well when I met him on the opening day of my son's camping period. Winning that flag for keeping the latrine clean seemed to mean so much to him. What a pity he had to relinquish it the following week. He will just have to get used to spirited boys, won't he?

I've been meaning to share with you some of my son's hilarious reports of your camp. He wrote us that when a boy talked after lights out, the boys got to slug him, and when he continued to talk, the counselor slugged him. I ask you, where would we be without a boy's imagination?

Incidentally, this is probably an oversight, but he has never received his camp award for throwing a frozen pancake thirty-two feet high. I understand from him this is some kind of a camp record. (Even if he was aiming it at a senior leader during evening meditation.) Although we are not "showy" people, we do have a spot for it in the trophy case in the hallway, alongside his birth certificate and a note saying he passed his eye test at school—his two accomplishments to date.

Did you ever solve the mystery of the missing bathing suits from camp? My son was terribly upset about the nude swimming as he is a sensitive boy.

Do write me your confirmation of my son's registration.
    Sincerely

Dear Mrs. Bombeck:

We do remember your son.

Mr. Bley continues to improve and now is permitted a limited number of visitors on Sundays. We are enclosing your son's camp award and are sorry for the oversight.

The mystery of the missing bathing suits was solved soon after we searched your son's foot locker.

Registrations have been filled since just before Thanksgiving.

> Sincerely,
> Grim Gruber, Director
> Camp Discouragement for Boys

Nagging—American Style

AS THE BRIDE in the newspaper account told the police the other day after she shot her new husband at their wedding reception, "No marriage is perfect."

After I had read the story and had gone beyond the point of wondering why she was wearing a gun to her wedding, I got to wondering why she had shot him so soon. Surely they didn't have the time to approach the big problems that psychologists are always warning us about like: communications, consideration, honesty, thoughtfulness, in-laws, money, and children. It had to be then a perfect "case" for what I have always contended. The biggest problems in a marriage are all those little pesky differences that drive you behind a locked door in the bathroom, to the sofa to spend the night, to Mother's studio couch, to the lake with the boys, to the nearest bar, or straight into the arms of the Avon lady. Nagging one another about the most inane things you can think of then becomes one of the few ways you can give vent to these differences.

I have always said half of the arguments in this country are caused by a simple little thing like a mosquito in the

bedroom. It's true. The trouble festers when it becomes evident two opposites have married (a) those who don't mind mosquitoes in the bedroom and (b) those who find it impossible to exist with mosquitoes in their bedroom.

Usually this discovery is not made until the first summer after marriage. When it happens, it's enough to make World War II sound like a wet cap pistol.

Generally, but not always, it's the woman who can't stand the sharp, whining buzz about her head. Promptly she will throw back the covers, illuminate the bedroom with light, stand in the middle of the bed and announce, "Clyde, we can't sleep with that mosquito in this bedroom. Clyde! Clyde! I say, we can't sleep with that mosquito in this bedroom."

Now, Clyde comes out of his unconscious state mumbling, "Hold him, Tom, while I get the net. You don't want to lose him at the boat. He looks like a three-pounder."

"Wake up," he is ordered. "You're not fishing. We're chasing a mosquito. Here, take this paper and don't miss!"

"Look," he pleads sleepily, "why don't you just ignore him and go to sleep. What's a small mosquito?"

"They're noisy and they carry malaria," she states flatly.

He groans, "With malaria I can stay home from work and get paid. Exhaustion, they won't buy."

"Wait a minute," she says excitedly, "I think he's in the bathroom. Quick, shut the door."

"Now, can I go back to bed?" he asks.

"No, I think there's a pair of them. This dizzy wallpaper. You can't see anything on it at night. I hate this wallpaper. Be still. He was on my pillow a while back. There he is . . . get him! You missed! For a man who can hit a baseball, a golf ball, and can fly cast into a circle, you're lousy at hitting mosquitoes."

"It's *your* mosquito, Great White Hunter, you kill it!" he says.

"And how did we get mosquitoes?" she retaliates. "I'll tell you how. They slip through your homemade screens."

"Well, they had to go on a diet to do it," he yells back.

"And another thing," she shouts. "Your mother had no right to wear navy blue to our wedding."

"You always bring that up," he informs her. "It has nothing to do with mosquitoes."

"How would you like to sleep in this disease-ridden jungle all by yourself?"

"I'd sleep in a crocodile's stomach to get that bright light out of my eyes," he blusters.

"Okay, Clyde," she storms. "That tore it. I'm going to the sofa for a decent night's sleep. If you want to chase mosquitoes all night, that's your business!"

Second only to the mosquito is the problem of the electric blanket. When electric blankets came out, some simple-minded designer hung a single control box on it and hoped for a miracle.

I defy you to put any blissfully happy married couple under a blanket with a single control and have them speaking to one another in the cold light of morning. Quite frankly, I haven't seen such a home wrecker since they legalized the Watusi.

Why only last week, a pair of my dearest friends, Wanda and Lester Blissful, separated over a single-control electric blanket. Naturally the card club doesn't have the full details yet, but the way we understand it, Wanda was readying for bed one night when Lester said gruffly, "Are you wearing that little sleeveless gown to bed?"

"I don't usually wear a snowsuit," she smiled stiffly. (Wanda's a real corker.)

"If you're planning on hiking that blanket up to a seven again tonight, forget it," he said firmly. "Last night, I slept like the FBI was trying to wring a confession out of me."

She smiled. "You exaggerate. I had the control on five. The night before you had it on two and I nearly froze. You know, Lester, if I had known you were a No. two on the electric blanket, I would never have married you. There's something wrong with a man who would let his veins freeze over."

This is all hearsay, mind you, but we heard they sniped at each other all night long. Lester said, "I feel a Mau Mau is having me for lunch . . . literally!" Wanda said, "That's better than feeling like a prime beef in a food locker!" Lester retaliated with "Toasted marshmallows, anyone?" Wanda shot back, "Welcome to Ski Valley."

After a sleepless night for both of them, they decided things weren't working out between them and they made an appointment with their lawyer.

Their properties, holdings, and children were divided with cold efficiency. There was no problem here. Then Lester spoke, "Who gets custody of the electric blanket?"

"What do you need it for?" yelled Wanda. "You could get the same cold feet by hanging them out of the window."

"And you could get equally warm by wetting your finger and sticking it into an electrical outlet!" he charged.

At this point the lawyer interceded and suggested they buy an electric blanket with dual controls. He said he and his wife would assume custody of the blanket with the single control.

Their case comes up next month, so they say at card club.

Very frankly, two things have nearly wrecked our marriage: a home freezer and the checking account. Now, I know what you're going to say. Right away, you're going to jump to the conclusion that I bought an expensive home freezer without telling my husband and that I abuse the checking account by spending too much money. You are wrong. They are just small things to "nag" about.

For example, we've been arguing about that home freezer for three years now. It's been paid for since a year ago last August. (In fact, I heard there was a Conga line at the credit office that snaked out to the elevator and that the manager treated the staff to cranberry juice out of paper cups, but that could be a rumor.)

At any rate, I insisted we buy the freezer because I couldn't live through another "harvest" without it. I wanted to preserve some of that fresh corn on the cob, green beans, melon balls, peaches, and strawberries. So, my husband agreed to the freezer.

The first week, I snapped and broke thirty pounds of green beans. I blanched them, cooled them, put them into plastic bags, then into boxes where I duly marked the date: June 5. By June 28 we had consumed thirty pounds of green beans. I went the same route with corn and carrots. No matter what quantities I put into the freezer, we had it eaten clean by the end of the week.

In the fall I bought a bushel of apples. I peeled, cored,

88

blanched, cooled, bagged, boxed, and labeled. The yield was eight quarts which someone figured cost me $2.33 a quart, counting labor. (On a rice-paddy minimum wage scale.)

One day my husband decided to check out the freezer. I held my breath. "Well now, what do we have on this shelf?" he asked quizzically.

"Snowballs," I said softly. "The kids made them up when it snowed and then when it's summer, we've got this wonderful, rich supply of snowballs that we couldn't possibly begin to have if we just had the freezing compartment in the refrigerator."

"And what are all those brown paper bags filled with? Steaks? Rump roasts? Chops?"

"You're warm," I said, slamming the door shut.

"How warm?" he asked, opening it again.

"Chicken innards," I said.

"*Chicken innards!*"

"That's right," I explained. "You always said I wasn't to put them into the garbage can until the day of pick-up and I thought I could store them in the freezer until garbage day. I guess I forgot to put a few of them out."

"Is this what I think it is?" he asked tiredly.

"It is, I believe, a transistor battery. Someone said if you put them in a freezer, they'd recharge themselves."

"So, this is what I gave up cigarettes for," he whimpered. "This is why I painted my heels black so no one would know I was wearing socks with holes in them. This is why I didn't buy a library card . . . just to save money. All for a frozen patch of snowballs, batteries, and chicken necks!"

"Aren't you being a little dramatic?"

"You are some kind of a nut," he accused. "It's a good thing they don't try to match you up in some computer, or you'd be married to Bert Lahr and living on a Funny Farm."

I'd like to say I filled the freezer to capacity with a hind quarter of whatever it is you freeze and we lived happily ever after. I'd like to say it, but I can't. I figured if we didn't argue about all those chicken innards, we might argue about something serious.

As for the checking account, it's simply a little thing about being "neat." The first year we were married, we opened our first checking account. My first entries looked like the work of a monastery monk. They were bold and black, lettered evenly, and stood out in complete legibility.

As the months wore on I began to scribble, abbreviate, and write notes in the margin. Then I would rearrange deposits and dates with bent arrows. Finally, my husband said one day, "I am going to start you in a nice new bank tomorrow. Would you like that? Your checks will start with No. one again and your ledger will be spanking clean."

The next bank was the same story, only they had no sense of humor for my notes attached to the checks. ("Luvie, hang on to this one until Monday. Our new money isn't dry yet.") We pushed on to another bank and another account.

In time, I began to shop for banks like a new home owner. I can tell you in a flash which banks have dry inkwells, which ones sell bookends, and which ones flaunt lollipop trees and pastel checks. At one establishment I received a nasty note advising me to sign my name the way I signed it on the records. My husband was visibly annoyed with me. "How did you sign your name originally?" he queried.

"Alf Landon," I said.

He collapsed in a chair and it served him right for doubting me.

Another time they became quite oral about the omission of my account number. There followed another inquisition. "Well, what number *did* you use?" I tried to remember. "I think it was my social security number . . . or my oil company number . . . or my swimming club number . . . or was it my record club?"

Things did go a little better when my husband figured out

90

my checkbook abbreviations. For example, NS beside an entry meant "No Stamp" to mail the check. Thus that check would be re-entered as a deposit and added on to the total. An OOB meant "Out Of Balance" and was the amount the bank and I differed. Thus, a subtraction and we began even again.

FB was entered when the item was so frivolous and ridiculous I knew he'd raise the roof if he knew. It stood for "Fringe Benefits." Others took some explanation. "What's this entry for Nursery—seventy-one dollars? We haven't had a baby in eight years," he growled.

"Geraniums," I said.

"Seventy-one dollars worth of geraniums!"

"Oh, of course not, ninny, that bill was for seventeen dollars. I made a mistake and transposed the numbers and I had to record the check like I wrote it. I only subtracted seventeen dollars though because the nursery wouldn't cash a check for seventy-one dollars. No one buys that many geraniums." We were overdrawn and moved on to another bank.

To date, I have been in more banks than Jesse James. But I figure if my husband wanted a financial giant, he should have shopped a little longer and not snatched the first skirt to come down the pike.

I suppose I should condemn marital nagging, but I'm not going to.

The American Institute of Family Relations observed a while back there are three times during a day when wifely nagging is the most dangerous: at breakfast, before dinner, and again at bedtime.

So what's left? A spontaneous argument can be rather stimulating after a morning playing "Red Goose Run" with Captain Kangaroo. It picks up tired blood, clears the old sinuses, sharpens the reflexes, and gives you a chance to use words like: insidious, subversive, ostentatious, incarceration, ambiguous, partisan, incumbent, and other words which you don't

91

know the meaning of either, but which you're reasonably sure are fit for children to hear.

Besides, it's a challenge. There's a sameness to nagging that occurs after you've been married awhile. The routines became as familiar as the dialogue of two vaudevillians. My husband has one called "Where's the table salt?" or as the kids call it, "The Great American Tragedy." I could serve eagle eyeballs under glass, wearing a topless bathing suit, and he'd shout, "What does a man have to do to get salt to his table!"

I have some old standards that I replay from time to time. There're "This house is a penal institution," "I didn't know you were allergic to grass when I married you," and "Why is it other men look like a page out of a Sears catalogue and you drag around in baggy pants like Hans Brinker?"

A little nagging is a healthy thing in a marriage. The way I figure it, you can either nag your way through fifty or sixty years or wear a gun to your wedding.

july 10 — september 5

what's a mother for
but to suffer?

OF ALL THE EMOTIONS enjoyed by a mother, none makes her feel as wonderfully ignoble as her "What's a Mother For But to Suffer?" period.

It doesn't happen in a day, of course. She has to build up to it through a series of self-inflicted tongue wounds. She observes, for example, "I could be St. Joan of Arc with the flames licking around my ankles, and Harlow would roast marshmallows." Or, "If I were on the *Titanic* and there was only one seat left in the lifeboat, Merrill would race me for it." Finally, at the peak of her distress, she will sum up her plight thusly, "I could be lying dead in the street and Evelyn would eat a peanut butter sandwich over me."

The image of her own sacrifice and thankless devotion to motherhood grows and grows until finally she is personified in every little old lady who scrubs floors at night to send a son through law school to every snaggle-toothed hag who sells violets in the snow.

Outwardly most women are ashamed of this emotion. They are loathe to admit that a small child, born of love, weaned on innocence, and nurtured with such gentleness could frustrate them to such cornball theatrics. They blame society, the educational system, the government, their mother, their obstetrician, their husband, and Ethel Kennedy for not telling them what motherhood was all about. They weren't prepared and they're probably bungling the whole process of child-rearing.

They just took a few of "what Mother always saids" and stirred in a generous portion of "what Daddy always dids" and said a fervent prayer that the kids didn't steal hubcaps while they were trying to figure out what they were going to do.

I've always blamed my shortcomings as a mother on the fact that I studied Child Psychology and Discipline under an unmarried professor whose only experience was in raising a dog. He obviously saw little difference.

At the age of two, my children could fetch and I'd reward them with a biscuit. At the age of four, they could sit, heel, or stay just by listening to the inflection in my voice. They were paper trained by the age of five. It was then that I noted a difference between their aims and goals and mine. So I put away my Child Psychology and Discipline volume and substituted a dog-eared copy of *Crime and Punishment*. I am now the only mother in our block who reaches out to kiss her children and has them flinch and threaten to call their attorneys if I so much as lay a finger on them.

Then a friend of mine told me she had a solution that worked pretty well. It was "Wait until your father gets home." This seemed to be working for me, too. It certainly took away the "acid stomach condition" that had been so bothersome. But one afternoon I heard the children making plans to either give Daddy up for Lent or lend him to a needy boy at Christmas and I felt a twinge of conscience.

We talked it over—their father and I—and finally conceded child-raising was a two-headed job, literally speaking. We would have to share the responsibilities. We have a list of blunders that span Diana Dors twice, not the least being our stab at sex education.

The sex education of a child is a delicate thing. None of us wants to "blow it." I always had a horror of ending up like the woman in the old joke who was asked by her child where he came from and after she explained the technical process in a well-chosen medical vocabulary, he looked at her intently and said, "I just wondered. Mike came from Hartford, Connecticut."

My husband and I talked about it and we figured what better way to explain the beautiful reproduction cycle of life than through the animal kingdom. We bought two pairs of guppies and a small aquarium. We should have bought two pairs of guppies and a small reservoir. Our breakfast conversation eventually assumed a pattern.

"What's new at Peyton Place by the Sea?" my husband would inquire.

"Mrs. Guppy is e-n-c-e-i-n-t-e again," I'd say.

"Put a little salt in the water. That'll cure anything," he mumbled.

"Daddy," said our son. "That means she's pregnant!"

"Again!" Daddy choked. "Can't we organize an intramural volleyball team in there or something?"

The first aquarium begat a second aquarium with no relief in sight.

"Are you getting anything out of your experience with guppies?" I asked my son delicately one afternoon. "Oh yeah," he said, "they're neat."

"I mean, have you watched the male and the female? Do you understand the processes that go into the offspring? The role of the mother in all this?"

"Oh sure," he said. "Listen, how did you know which one of your babies to eat when they were born?"

97

We added a third aquarium which was promptly filled with salt water and three pairs of sea horses.

"Now, I want you to pay special attention to the female," I instructed. "The chances are it won't take her long to be with child and perhaps you can see her actually give birth."

"The female doesn't give birth, Mom," said my son peeling a banana. (I felt myself smiling, anticipating a trend.) "Ridiculous," I said. "Females always give birth." The male began to take on weight. I thought I saw his ankles swell. He became a mother on the twenty-third of the month.

"That's pretty interesting," observed my son. "I hope when I become a mother, it's on land. I can't tread water that long."

We blew it. We figured we would.

If you want to know the truth, we haven't made out too well in the problem of sibling rivalry either. I think the rumor is that more parents have been driven out of their skulls by sibling rivalry than any other behavior phase. I started the rumor.

In infancy, it's a series of small things. Big sister will stuff a whole banana in the mouth of baby brother with the threat, "Shut your mouth, baby, or out you go." Or big brother will slap his toddler sister off her hobby horse with the reprimand, "Keep that squeak on your side of the room." It eventually reaches a point where they are measuring their cut of meat with a micrometer to see they are getting their fair share as set down by the Geneva Convention, and being represented by legal counsel to see who gets the fruit cocktail with the lone cherry on top.

The rivalry of each day, however, seems to culminate at the dinner table.

SON: She's doing it again.
FATHER: Doing what?
SON: Humming.

DAUGHTER: I am not humming.

SON: You are so. There, she did it again, Dad. Watch her neck. She's humming so no one can hear her but me. She does it all the time just to make fun of me.

FATHER: I can't hear anything. Eat your dinner.

SON: How come *he* got the bone?

FATHER: What difference does it make? There's no meat on the bone, anyway.

OTHER SON: Then how come *he* got the meat? I got stuck with the bone the last time.

DAUGHTER: I got dibs on the last black olive. *You* got the ice cube in your water after school and *you* got the bike for your birthday, so I get the black olive.

FATHER: What kind of logic is that! I swear it's like eating with the mafia. (*Turning to Mother*) How can you sit there and listen to all this drivel?

MOTHER: I'm under sedation.

This seemed to be the answer until recently, when some dear friends of ours confided in us that they had all but solved their sibling rivalry problems at the dinner table. We listened to them talk of peace, love, and tranquility throughout the meal by engaging in a new game called Category. It worked very simply. Each member of the family was allowed one night at the table where he alone named the Category and led that particular discussion. Hence, everyone had a chance to speak and sooner or later each child could talk about something that interested him.

I had to admit, Category sounded like a better game than we were playing at present called Trials at Nuremberg. This also worked rather simply. We would wait until we were all assembled at the table, then right after the prayer we'd confront the children with crimes they had committed in their playpens up to the present day. We'd touch upon bad manners, bicycles in the driveway, socks under the bed, goofing around with the garbage detail, throwing away their allow-

ances on paraffin teeth and anything else we could document. By the time we reached dessert, we usually had a couple of them sobbing uncontrollably into their mashed potatoes, begging to be sent to an orphanage. We decided to give Category a try.

"Tonight, I'm going to talk about 'Friends,'" said our older son.

"Don't talk with food in your mouth," amended his father.

He swallowed and continued, "My very best, first choice, A-1 top of the list, first class, Cadillac of a friend is Charlie."

"Charlie who?" someone interrupted.

"I don't know his last name," he shrugged. "Just Charlie."

"Well, good grief," I sighed. "You'd certainly think if you had a big, fat Damon and Pythias relationship with a real, live friend you'd get around to last names."

"Who's Damon and Pythias?" asked a small voice.

"Aw, come on," said the speaker. "It's not your turn until tomorrow night. Anyway, today my best friend, Charlie, threw up in school—"

100

"*Mother!*" screamed a voice. "Do I have to sit here and listen to stories about Charlie up-chucking?"

"Tell us about another friend, son," pleaded his father.

He continued. "Well, my second best B-2, second from the top of the list, Oldsmobile of a friend is Scott. Today, Scott went after the janitor to bring the bucket when Charlie threw up and—"

"Please!" the entire table groaned.

"Well, it's my category," he insisted, "and they're my friends. If I have to sit and listen to you talk about your junk, you can listen to me."

"I wish Charlie were here to eat these cold mashed potatoes."

"Yeah, well, when it's your turn to talk, I'm going to hum."

"All right, kids," interrupted their father. "While we're on the subject of cold mashed potatoes, who left the red bicycle right in the middle of the driveway tonight? And, as long as we're all together, which one of you lost the nozzle off the garden hose? (*Aside*) Hold up the dessert, Mother, I've got a few things to discuss. Now, about the telephone. I'm getting a little sick and tired of having to shinny up the pole every time I want to call out . . ."

Very frankly, I don't feel the problem of sibling rivalry will ever be worked out in our time. Especially after reading a recent survey taken among brothers and sisters as to what they liked or disliked about one another. These were some of the reasons for their contempt of one another. "He's my brother." "She says hello to me in front of my friends." "She's a girl." "He's always hanging around the house when I'm there." "She acts big and uppity." "She's a sloppy beast." "He knows everything." Only one brother said something nice about his sister. He wrote, "Sometimes when she takes a bath, she uses a neat deodorant." I ask you, how are you going to build a quiet meal around that!

The second-largest problem to parents is status. It changes

101

from year to year, beginning with "I'm five years old and *my* mama lets me stay up to watch the late, late show," to "I'm in the sixth grade too and I'm listed in the phone book under my own name."

It gets pretty ridiculous, of course, but it's just another hair-shirt in a mother's wardrobe. Another challenge for a mother who must make a decision not to measure her own children's happiness with another mother's yardstick. Just last month, I heard that the lastest status symbol around the bridge table is children's dental work. Wild? Not really. The more fillings, the more space maintainers, the more braces, the more status. If the orthodontist says your kid has a bite problem, lady, you're in.

Here's a conversation I overheard illustrating the point.

"You talk about dental work," said a small blonde. "Come here, George. Open your mouth, George." The lights danced on George's metal-filled mouth like Ali Baba's cave. "That," she said emphatically, "is my mink stole. A mother's sacrifice. And is he grateful? He is not."

"Think nothing of it," said her companion. "Come over here, Marcia. Let the lady look at your braces." Marcia mechanically threw back her head and opened wide. The inside of her mouth looked like it was set to go off. "That," she said, "is my trip to Europe. What do you think of that?"

"I think we worry too much about them," said the first one. "Always nagging. 'Brush your teeth, don't eat sweets.' I mean we can't run around after them like those hags on television, can we?"

"Wait till you see what I'm buying George for his mouth this month," the blonde confided. "You'll be dumbfounded. It's very new and expensive and I understand there aren't a half dozen people who have them in their mouths yet. George and I will be one of the first."

"What is it?" asked the first one breathlessly.

"Promise you won't tell anyone?" (*Hushed tone*) "It's a telltale tooth."

"A telltale tooth?"

"Right. They cram six miniature transmitters, twenty-eight other electrical components, and two rechargeable batteries into what looks like an ordinary 'bridge' of a first molar. Then, as they chew, the telltale tooth broadcasts a stream of information to the dentist that tells what the child has eaten and what is causing the breakdown of his teeth."

"A fink tooth! Well, I'll be. I think I'll get one of those for Marcia. Maybe we could hook up her transistor to it and do away with that wire coming out of her ear. Then the music could come from her teeth. Wouldn't that give the kids in her class a jolt!"

"Well, I thought I'd get an antenna for George's. Then maybe he could hook up to that Early Bird channel from Telestar and draw in something from overseas."

"There goes that patio cover you were saving for—but then, what's a mother for, but to sweat in the hot sun."

A mother's suffering—a privilege or a put-upon. Who knows. I only know that when you can no longer evoke any empathy from your children with it, then you must take a firm stance, throw back your head, look determined, and as my old Child Psychology professor advised, "Pull up hard on the leash!"

Color Me Naïve

BOY, MAYBE I'M NAÏVE or something, but what's with these women who waddle into the hospital complaining of a bad case of indigestion and deliver twins two hours later? When presented with their case of indigestion swathed in pink blankets, they express shock and say, "I didn't even know I was pregnant!"

I'm the suspicious type. I think when they got to the stage

where they couldn't see their feet over their stomachs, couldn't fit behind a car steering wheel, couldn't wear anything but a tent with a drawstring neckline, they suspected, all right.

Granted, some women show less than others during pregnancy, but the only women I know who actually carry babies "concave" are magazine models and television actresses. And I never saw one of them I didn't hate! What they do is they nail these fashion models in the second week of their pregnancy, pour them into a Paris original and try to convince Mrs. Housewife that even models have babies and they don't look like Humpty Dumpty with a grouch.

Television is worse. On soap operas, for example, the actress rarely gets out of her street clothes. Oh, she may complain of a backache, tiredness, nausea, and swollen ankles, but the straight skirts and severe sheaths continue. I have also noted the length of pregnancies on a soap opera is no more than eight or nine weeks, a decided improvement over the standard nine months. Finally, in the ninth week (when they have padded her with a cotton swab) she complains of labor. She is fresh from the beauty shop and is ready to deliver. The baby is never seen. She (a) loses it, (b) puts it up for adoption, or (c) never wants to see it again. This creates fewer problems for casting.

You can expect such an unrealistic approach from medias that deal in make-believe, but in real life it would sound like an old William Powell-Myrna Loy movie.

MYRNA: William, I should have told you before, but we're going to have a baby.

WILLIAM: (*The match he is holding burns his fingers.*) A baby, but when?

MYRNA: Tomorrow.

WILLIAM: But why didn't you tell me, my dear?

MYRNA: I was afraid you'd be cross with me. Are you surprised?

WILLIAM: I can't believe it. So that's why there's a baby crib in our bedroom . . . and I've been cooking all the meals . . . and your suitcase is packed . . . it's all beginning to make sense now. But how was I to know? Day after day I'd find you just sitting in that chair.

MYRNA: I can't get out of it.

WILLIAM: Could I get you something? A glass of water? An obstetrician?

MYRNA: Just a helping hand out of this chair. (*She stands up, forty-five pounds heavier than she was nine months ago, shoulders flung back, feet apart.*) There now, be honest, didn't you suspect something?

WILLIAM: Nonsense. You still look like the bride I married.

I recently became very interested in the story of a London housewife who was at odds with English automobile manufacturers over the low position of steering wheels for expectant mothers who have to drive a car. The automobile

105

manufacturers retaliated with "Why should pregnant women have to drive at all?" which is the type of answer you'd expect from a bachelor engineer whose mommy told him she got him with green stamps!

Actually, pregnant women don't have to drive cars. They could ride motorcycles sidesaddle, strap their feet to two skateboards, or raise their umbrellas and think Mary Poppins, but the fact remains automobiles are an intricate part of a woman's life and to give them up for six months or so is like going back to nesting in a rocking chair for nine months.

I know of what I speak. Before American cars were equipped with tilt-away steering wheels, I had a traumatic experience that I have not been able to relate to more than thirty or forty thousand of my most intimate friends.

I was going into my eleventh month of pregnancy (the doctor and I disagreed on this point) and had gone to the store to purchase a half gallon of ice cream and a loaf of bread. The car seat was back as far as it would go, which created a small problem. My feet no longer reached the brake pedal or the accelerator, so I had to crouch. When I crouched, my vision was impaired and I had to hang my head out of the no-draft. When I did this, I hit things.

No matter. I got to the store and parked the car, nose in, and made my exit without incident. However, on my return I noticed I had been hemmed in on both sides by parked cars.

I eased open the door a crack and proceeded to stuff myself into the car, stomach first. However, I became wedged between the arm rest of the door and the steering wheel. I could not go forward or backward. Now, try that on for laughs. My stomach was stuck and my ice cream was melting.

People began to stand around in curious mobs. Quickly I pulled backward, releasing me from the front seat. To save face, I nonchalantly opened the back door of the car and slid in like a guest. Now, to get to the front seat. Bent from the waist, I faced the rear of the car and tried rolling over the top of the front seat. The ashtray tore a hole in my bread wrapper.

Humiliated, I plopped down on the seat to think. What do you do when you go to the supermarket manager and ask him to announce over his microphone that the black station wagon bearing license plates ——— is blocking *a stomach?* I licked the sticky ice cream off my fingers and decided to give it one more try. I'd back into the front seat. I was doing fine until another fat part of me made contact with the horn. A small child pointed and said, "Mommy, is that woman sitting on her horn going to have a baby?"

Tears welled in my eyes. "Don't be ridiculous, kid! I'm carrying it for a dear friend."

Whenever I'd get really depressed over my plight, I'd think about a footnote I read once in a Population Study Patterns report. (I picked that up in a doctor's office. It beat reading *Gall Bladder Digest.*) It said an Austrian woman had set an "apparent world population record" by bearing sixty-nine offspring. What's more, she did it the government way: in carbons and triplicates. Here's her tally.

BIRTHS	SETS	TOTALS
Quadruplets	4	16
Triplets	7	21
Twins	16	32
	TOTAL:	69

I used to think about her a lot. Without ever having set eyes on her, you can tell many things from these figures. Obviously this is a woman who hates the pesky details of packing a suitcase. You'll note she made only twenty-seven trips to the maternity ward. Likewise, she's a woman who doesn't waste time in repetition. If she had felt a single birth coming, she would probably haved phoned it in.

107

She's a person used to looking upward, not having seen her feet in twenty-seven years. Heartburn to her is a way of life, while a knit suit is as unreal as Santa Claus. In all probability, her sense of humor has been dulled. When she and her husband planned their marriage in the first full bloom of courtship, and he proposed, "We'll have thirty-one boys for me and thirty-eight girls for you," she probably blushed and said, "You're a regular card, Stanley."

As she tallied up the twenty-ninth, thirtieth, and thirty-first births, undoubtedly "Tell Mother we're expecting again" became a rather dreary chore. After arrivals forty-three, forty-four, and forty-five, she probably had reached the yellow pages of the phone book for names and was reduced to calling number forty-six the Aufderheiden Bottling Company. Upon the birth of fifty-one and fifty-two, the problem of how to get to thirty-seven PTA Open Houses likely threw them. When the children reached the sixties, it was undoubtedly a strain to remember not whose birthday was Saturday, but how many.

I can visualize many problems with sixty-nine children in the house. Taking numbers to get into the bathroom, getting your clothes issued from a quartermaster, substituting the word "invasion" for "visit" and tactfully suggesting to two redheads they've been sleeping with the wrong family for three years.

The story goes on to reveal that the average woman has a potential capability of producing something like twenty offspring, discounting the possibility of multiple births. (If that doesn't make your day, it's beyond help.) So, if you stand now at the national average, which is 2.7 children per family, you and your husband are going to have to go some to make a footnote out of yourself!

No story on motherhood these days is complete without mention of two static words, "The Pill." I'm inclined to go along with the sign on a diaper service truck I saw last week. As it whizzed through town at a law-breaking speed, I caught the sign painted on its rear doors, "What Pill?"

Actually, there are two things in this country directly opposing The Pill, both birds.

First, Europeans are staging an all-out effort to increase the population of the storks. To keep them from becoming extinct, sympathetic French citizens are keeping them in their kitchens to protect them from cold snaps, an emergency stork committee has been named to make sure the birds survive the hazards of high-tension wires and television antennae, and at one point an airlift was staged to transport young birds from Algeria to France. And how do you think these grateful birds will repay the French citizens for their hospitality? By moving on to Chicago, Los Angeles, New York, Denver, and Philadelphia, what else?

Frankly I'm pretty jittery about the whole deal. I get panicky when I see a dove fly in Clara's window.

The other bird who is blocking the breakthrough of The Pill to American women is the pigeon. With the projected people population running into the billions, overcrowded schools, limited housing, lack of food and threat of unemployment, the birth control pill was awarded by the government to the pigeons so that they could control their numbers.

I suppose if you're a pedestrian who walks under high window ledges, this might have some meaning for you, but I don't think the pigeons were even seeking assistance from the government.

Crawling out on a rather narrow ledge of the courthouse, I talked recently with a spokesman—the only bird who knew pigeon English—about the talked-about Pill.

"Well, if people don't want us around, why don't they say so?" he cooed. "I'm sick of this shilly-shallying. When we first moved from the suburbs into the cities, the natives took potshots at us. Of course, they were severely criticized by the ASPCA—not the barbershop harmony group, dear, the Society for the Prevention of Cruelty to Animals.

"Next, they tried a variety of insecticides to make us leave

109

our perches. Finally, they put electrical charges on the buildings where we walk. And if you think that doesn't give you a jolt when you set down for a landing, you haven't changed radio stations while you were in the bathtub lately.

"No, I think they've gone too far. Oh, I suppose we do produce at a rather astounding rate. But there's nothing else to do up here all day long but fly over parked cars and mess around the statues in the parks."

I asked him how the women of this country should go about getting The Pill.

"All I can offer is some advice on how we got to be a menace. We just made our numbers felt in the downtown area."

"I'll tell them," I said.

The more I think of it, however, the more I'm convinced that fertility, or the lack of it, doesn't depend on a pill, a chart, or a clinic. It rests solely with the predisposition of women.

For example, go buy a new bathing suit, go on a diet, invest twenty dollars in a pair of stretch pants so tight you can trace your lunch and *voilà!* Pregnancy! Or more drastic measures: Let your Blue Cross lapse, buy a small sports car with two bucket seats, or adopt a baby. You asked for it. Instant parenthood.

If you're really serious about limiting your family, you should follow the following advice:

1. Young mothers are urged to hang on to maternity clothes, sterilizers, bottle warmers, beds, baby tenders, sheet blankets, pads, and reusable pacifiers. If storage space is needed, dig a hole under the house if necessary.

2. Don't make vacation plans in September for the next summer at Lake Erie or in New York. Clinical records have indicated women who planned to scale the inside of the Statue of Liberty were so pregnant by vacation time they were lucky the ferryboat didn't capsize.

110

3. Resist the impulse to sign up for self-improvement courses in the daytime or academic study at the university in the evening. This is a sure way to get back to testing strained liver with the tip of your tongue.

4. Do not be tempted by the job markets until you are beyond sixty. Remember. Roads to fertility begin at the employment office—especially for those who make a big deal inquiring about vacations and retirement benefits.

5. Keep a keen eye on budget spending. Deferred accounts, long-term credit buying is like waving a red flag before the odds.

6. Don't become too enamored with water sports such as expensive boats, water skiing, and scuba diving. This could be awkward and limiting later on.

7. Don't make any public speeches over bridge tables on topics such as, "I named my last one Caboose. And that's it!" or "Did you hear about Fanny and she's forty-two!"

I may be naïve, but I'm no fool!

The Disenchanted

SOME WOMAN once nailed me in a restroom in Detroit and said, "I can hardly wait until your children are a little older. You will have such fun writing about them during that stage." The woman, an obvious sadist who hangs around restrooms and stirs up trouble, never mentioned the precise age at which child-rearing got to be a fun thing. I am still waiting.

When the children were quite young, I used to envision a time when they would gather at my feet and say, "Now don't you lift an arthritic finger, Mother. I know exactly where your pinking shears are. Let me run and get them for you." Frankly I cannot remember a time when our popularity as parents has been at such an all-time low.

111

Our children barricade themselves behind locked bedroom doors, emerging only when the telephone rings. The "phono-mania" is probably our doing. We noted long ago that some of our friends had a real phone problem with their children. (One couple had the run of the phone from 4 to 6:30 A.M. weekdays only, during the months with R in them.) So we decided that when our children were old enough to point to the telephone and say, "Mommy, what is that?" we'd answer, "It's a cavity machine to check the cavities in your teeth." (We also told them steak made little children sick, but that is another story.) Our yarn about the cavity machine began to leak holes when our daughter discovered by lifting the handle of the cavity machine and dialing a few numbers she could be in touch with thousands of cavity machines throughout the world. She has had a Princess phone stuck in her ear ever since.

The key word with growing children—are there any other kind?—seems to be communication. If you're a lip-reader of any repute whatsoever, you have no problem. However, if you must compete with local disc jockeys which feed hourly through their earplugs this could get pretty sticky. We have solved this problem by buying time on the local station and reporting personal messages: "We moved last week." "Daddy's birthday is in September." "Do you still lisp?"

Naturally you can't live among all those decibels and not be affected by it. I didn't know how noise could become a way of life until the other day when I answered the door and a young man said, "Pardon me, madam, I'm doing a survey among mothers to see whether or not they agree with an acoustical engineer from Arizona that rock 'n' roll may cause teenagers to go deaf."

"No, I don't need any rolls or bread today. If you've got any of those little buns with the jelly inside, though—"

"No, madam," he said, raising his voice, "you don't understand. I'm not a bakery man. I'd like to get your opinion on what hearing experts are saying about rock 'n' roll music and whether or not you think excessive—"

"*Oh, Excedrin!* You want me to do a commercial? My yes, I have headaches all the time. It's this loud music. You see, we've got four radios in the house. Along about four o'clock it sounds like the U. N. General Assembly singing a serenade in four languages to Red China. I simply crawl under the sink with a shaker full of Excedrin and—"

"Madam," he said facing me squarely, "we're not doing a commercial. We're doing a survey. Do you have a teenager in your home?"

"You're going to have to keep your lips in full view of my eyes at all times," I explained. "And talk a little slower."

"I'm sorry," he said. "Do you have a teenager in your home?"

"I think that's what it is," I said hesitantly. "The bangs are two inches above the hemline and there's a lump on the hip shaped like a small transistor, two button eyes, and a long cord that connects the hip to the ear."

"That's a teenager," he added impersonally. "Now, have you noticed any impairment in her hearing since she started listening to rock 'n' roll music?"

I pondered. "Nothing unusual. She still doesn't respond to simple commands like 'Clean your room,' 'Change your clothes,' 'Get the door.' On the other hand she picks up phrases like 'Have you heard the story about . . .' 'The bank balance is down to . . .' and 'Let's feed the kids early and slip out to dinner . . .' like she was standing in the middle of the Capitol rotunda in Washington."

"Then you have noticed that increased decibels have made a change in your teenager?"

"Pardon me while I get the phone."

"I didn't hear anything," he said.

"It's always like that after I've listened to three hours of Maurice and His Electric Fuse Boxes. Did you know that group once recorded the guitar player's hiccups and sold two million records? Are you saying something, young man? I told you you'd have to keep your lips in full view of my eyes at all times. *And speak a little slower!*"

Other than noise, possibly nothing is more perplexing to parents than the current hair styles. In our family it all began when our daughter said she was going to let her hair grow. Like a fool I thought she meant down her back! Little did I dream it would cascade over her face and that only a slight part in the middle would stand between her and asphyxiation.

Quite frankly the whole thing got on my nerves. "Are you awake under there?" I'd ask, my eyes squinting for a peek of flesh. "If you are, just rap twice on the table." Sometimes when the hair wouldn't move for a while, I'd get panicky and take her pulse. Then a voice would come out of the hair, "Mother! Please! I'm on the phone." For all I knew she could have had a ouija board and another friend in there with her. Occasionally she would style her hair in such a way that a single eye would be exposed. The eye would follow me about the room, not moving and rarely blinking. I often found myself addressing remarks to it.

One day when I came to the conclusion that she looked more like a troll than a human, I ventured a wild suggestion, "Why don't you cut your hair?"

I saw the hair part and a pair of lips emerge and say, "You've got to be kidding! I'd be the laughingstock of the school. No one cuts their hair anymore."

I saw my chance and took it. "That's it. Be a pace setter. Dare to be different. There is absolutely nothing more fresh and feminine in this world than short-cropped, clean hair with a little curl in the end and a little side bang. I tell you, you'd stand out like a pom pom girl in St. Petersburg, Florida. For the first time in your life, dare to look like a girl."

She pondered it for three weeks. Then her eyes glistening

114

with sentiment, she was sheared and was once again able to distinguish light from darkness. I admit I was pretty proud of myself. "You really look the way a young lady should look. I wouldn't be surprised if all the girls in your school followed your lead. It's so girlish . . . so ladylike . . . so feminine."

We were both standing in line at the local hamburger emporium when we heard it. An elderly couple quite frankly stared at my daughter's tapered slacks, boots, short jacket, and cropped hair for a full three minutes. Then they clucked, "Look at that boy! It's disgusting! What kind of a mother would let him dress like that!"

I will be glad when the hair grows back in again. Then I will only have one sad eye to follow me about.

Truly I wish I could collar that woman in Detroit and ask her when I get to laugh. Maybe it was the other night when the kids were talking with one another at the dinner table and they began to spell in front of us. Maybe it was when I overheard one of them asking their father if he wasn't a little old for a button-down collar. Or maybe it was when one of them shot me down for saying hello to them on the playground in front of their friends.

A parent gets a lot of theories these days on how they should raise their children. Treat them as children. Treat them as adults. Treat them as equals. Treat them as pals. Okay, when my children stop telling me Doris Day is three years older than I am and looks ten years younger, I'll consider them as associates. Until then, when do I get to laugh?

Reflections at Summer's End

THE END OF SUMMER is to me like New Year's Eve. I sense an end to something carefree and uninhibited, sandy and warm, cold and melting, barefoot and tanned. And yet I look forward with great expectation to a beginning of

115

schedules and appointments, bookbinders with little tabs, freshly sharpened pencils, crisp winds, efficiency, and routine.

I am sadly aware of a great rushing of time as I lengthen skirts and discard sweaters that hit above the wristbones. Time is moving and I want to stop it for just a while so that I may snatch a quiet moment and tell my children what it is I want for them and what all the shouting has been about.

The moment never comes, of course. I must compete with Captain Kangaroo, a baseball game, a Monkee record, a playmate, a cartoon or a new bike in the next block. So, I must keep these thoughts inside . . .

Too fast . . . you're moving too fast. Don't be in such a hurry to trade formulas for formals. You're going to own your own sports car before you've tried to build one out of orange crates and four baby buggy wheels. You're going to explore the world before you've explored the wonders of your own back yard. You're going to pad with cotton what the Good Lord will provide if you are just patient.

Don't shed your childhood like a good coat that's gotten a little small for you. A full-term childhood is necessary as is all phases of your growth. Childhood is a time for pretending and trying on maturity to see if it fits or hangs baggy, tastes good or bitter, smells nice or fills your lungs with smoke that makes you cough. It's sharing licks on the same sucker with your best friend before you discover germs. It's not knowing how much a house cost, and caring less. It's going to bed in the summer with dirty feet on clean sheets. It's thinking anyone over fifteen is "ancient." It's absorbing ideas, knowledge, and people like a giant sponge. Childhood is where "competition" is a baseball game and "responsibility" is a paper route.

I want to teach you so much that you must know to find happiness within yourself. Yet, I don't know where to begin or how.

I want you to be a square. That's right, a square! I want

you to kiss your grandmother when you walk into a room even if you're with friends. I want you to be able to talk openly of God and your love for Him. I want you to lend dignity to the things you believe in and respect for the things you don't believe in. I want you to be a human being who needs friends, and in turn deserves them. I want you to be a square who polishes his shoes, buttons the top button of his shirt occasionally, and stands straight and looks people in the eye when they are talking to you. There is a time to laugh and a time to cry. I want you to know the difference.

I want you to be a cornball, a real, honest-to-God, flag-waving cornball, who, if you must march, will tell people what you are for, not what you are against. I'm so afraid in your ultimate sophistication of growing up, you'll look upon Betsy Ross as a chairman who needed a service project, upon Barbara Frietchie as a senile who should have been committed to an institution by her son, upon the little old man who doffed his hat as the flag went by as the town drunk who never missed a parade.

Please cry when school children sing "The Battle Hymn of the Republic," when you see a picture of the Berlin Wall, when you see the American flag on the silver suit of an astronaut. Maybe I'm in a panic for nothing. It just seems that during the last few years the flag has become less symbolic to people. I think all of last year I only read two stories concerning a flag: one was about a flag being burned in front of a foreign embassy, the other involved an undergarment manufacturer who was under fire from the DAR for daring to make panties out of the Stars and Stripes. Have some feeling for it and for what it stands for. Wear it on you as big as a conventioneer's badge.

Please remember to have compassion. It's funny, a mother rarely forgets the first time her child leaves his small, self-centered world and thinks of someone other than himself. I remember when our youngest was six years old he came home from school one afternoon and demanded, "I need an old toothbrush and a toy truck."

"Don't tell me," I said laughing, "you're making a Thanksgiving centerpiece for the dining room table."

"Nope," he said proudly. "We're winning the war in Vietnam."

"With a toothbrush and a toy truck?"

"Mom," he said patiently, "you don't understand. Let me explain it to you. You see, we're fighting a war in a place called Vietnam and there are people over there who have nothing to brush their teeth with or anything. They don't need money. They just need toothbrushes. Can I have yours?"

"Well, don't you think we ought to send them a new one?"

"That's okay," he reasoned. "Now I have to pick out a truck . . . not one that's all beat up, but something a soldier would want to play with."

My eyes fairly popped out of my head. "A *soldier wants to play with!* You mean the Vietnamese children, don't you?"

118

Now his eyes widened. "You mean there are children in Vietnam? In the war?"

"Right in the middle of it," I explained. "Now go back and pick out a truck."

I found him sitting in the middle of the floor with a truck on his lap, preoccupied with his own thoughts. "I never thought there would be children in a war," he said.

"Few people do," I answered.

"Well, what do the children do all day while the soldiers fight?"

"Try to act like the war's not there."

"Do they play in another language?"

"No, it's a universal one."

"Will I be a soldier when I grow up?" he asked solemnly.

"I hope not. Why?"

"Because it's a crumby trick sending a neat package to a kid and having him open it and finding a silly toothbrush and someone's secondhand birthday truck. It's a rotten trick on a kid."

If I could only be sure all the lessons are sinking in and are being understood. How can I tell you about disappointments? You'll have them, you know. And they'll be painful, they'll hurt, they'll shatter your ego, lay your confidence in yourself bare, and sometimes cripple your initiative. But people don't die from them. They just emerge stronger. I want you to hear the thunder, so you can appreciate the calm. I want you to fall on your face in the dirt once in a while, so you will know the pride of being able to stand tall. Learn to live with the words "No! You can't! You're out! You blew it! I don't know." And "I made a mistake."

Adults are always telling young people, "These are the best years of your life." Are they? I don't know. Sometimes when adults say this to children I look into their faces. They look like someone on the top seat of the Ferris wheel who has had too much cotton candy and barbecue. They'd like to get off

119

and be sick but everyone keeps telling them what a good time they're having.

Do not imagine for a moment that I don't feel your fears and anxieties. Youth does not have an immunity from disappointments and heartbreaks. No one does.

Fears begin the day you were born: fear of baths, bed wetting, the dark, falling off the sink where you are being bathed, strangers throwing you into the air and not catching you, going hungry, noises, open pins.

Later, it's monsters, parents leaving and not coming back, death, hurts, and bad dreams. School only adds to anxieties. Fear of not having friends, being called upon and not knowing the answers, telling the truth when you're going to be punished, not getting to the bathroom in time, not being liked by a baby sitter, not loved by your parents when a new baby arrives in the house. As you mature, they continue to multiply. Fear of not achieving, not having friends, or not being accepted, not getting the car, worrying about war, marriage, career, making money, being attractive to the opposite sex and making the grades to graduate

Fears are normal. We all have them. Parents have the greatest fears of all. For we are responsible for this life which we have brought to this world. There is so much to teach and the time goes so fast . . .

Was that brisk draft of air a prelude to another fall, or did someone just rush by me in a hurry to turn on Captain Kangaroo?

Out of the Nest

WE CALL HIM "the baby."

He weighs forty pounds, stands stove-high and can kick a football higher than the house. Somehow, I have the feeling we will call him "the baby" when he is forty, has children of his own, and a hairline like the coast of Florida.

This day, in particular, is special. It's the day when "the baby" goes to school for the first time. I don't know why I feel so irritable. One minute I'm yelling at him, "You slam that door once more, fella, and I'll mail you to a school in Nebraska with no return address."

The next I'm scooping him to my bosom and saying, "Let's run away to Never-Never land, you and I, where little boys never grow up and I could get the job of Mother that Mary Martin gave up."

This should be a happy morning. I remember all those promises I made to myself while sloshing over diaper pails and shaking boiling hot milk over my wrists at 2 A.M. just six short years ago.

"Just wait," I told myself. "When this whole mess is behind me I'll go back to bed in the mornings, have lunch with someone who doesn't eat his meat with a spoon, shed fifteen pounds, do my nails, learn how to play bridge, and blow this firetrap called home that has held me a virtual prisoner."

I nurtured this dream through measles, fractures, tensions, traumas, Dr. Spock, and nursery school. And now that I am so close to realization, I feel guilty. What am I doing? Sending this "baby" off to learn calculus before the cord is healed. How can I possibly think of my own comforts when he is harboring all those insecurities? Indeed, how does the State of Ohio know my son is ready for the first grade? They look at him and what do they see? A birth certificate and a record of immunizations.

I look at him and I see a smile . . . like Halloween. I see two short legs that won't get him a drink of water without a stool under them. I see two pudgy hands that can't work together to hold a slippery bar of soap. I see a shock of red hair that doesn't come up to his father's belt buckle. I see a little boy who never went to the restroom all during nursery school because he didn't want to admit he couldn't spell the difference between B-O-Y-S from G-I-R-L-S on the door.

121

I should have prepared him more. I piffed away all that time on Santa Claus, Easter Bunny, Tooth Fairy, and Mary Poppins. I should've dealt with the basic realities like tolerance, forgiveness, compassion, and honesty. For from this day forward his world can only widen. An existence that began in a crib, grew to a house, and extends over a two-block bicycle ride will now go even beyond that. I will share him with another woman, other adults, other children, other opinions, other points of view. I am no longer leading. I am standing behind him ready to guide from a new position.

Who is this woman who will spend more daylight hours with him than I? Please, Miss Chalkdust or whatever, give him the patience and gentleness he needs. Please have a soft lap and a warm smile. Please don't be too pretty or too smart, lest I suffer from the comparison.

A note. Maybe I should pin a note on his sweater to make sure she understands you. I could say, "Dear Miss Chalkdust or whatever: I submit to your tender, loving care my son who is a little shy and a lot stubborn. Who can't cope yet with zippers that stick or buttons on sweaters that don't come out even. One who makes his 5's sideways but works seriously and in earnest. I may sue you for alienation of affection, but for the moment, God Bless You!"

Note. There is no time for a note. The bus is here. It's such a big bus. Why would they send their largest bus for someone so small? He is gone. He didn't even look back to wave.

Why was I so rotten to him all summer? I had five summers to be rotten to him and I had to concentrate all my rottenness into this one. It's funny when you think about it. You give six years of your life readying a child for school and all of a sudden you find you're being replaced by a stranger and a thirty-five-cent plate lunch.

The house is so quiet. It's what I've always wanted, isn't it? A quiet house. I wonder who my tears are really for. I hate to admit it, but I think they're for myself.

122

I think I'm afraid. What kind of a woman am I? Am I going to be the woman who wanders through the house, unfulfilled and bored, who occasionally plucks a pair of sticky socks off the ceiling and sobs into them, "My baby, my baby!"? Will I dust and vacuum the house every day and be tidied up by ten-thirty only to sit and drink coffee and watch for the big, yellow bus to deposit my brood at the curb that I may once again run and fetch like a robot that has been programmed for service?

Will my children go on being my crutch? My excuse for not stirring from this house? Will I dedicate my entire life to their comforts?

Or could I be like that robin in our spouting last spring? What a time to be thinking about robins in the spouting. I watched that little feathered mother-to-be all spring as she and her mate built the nest and she perched on her eggs to wait. Then, day of days, the babies were born and both she and the father scratched and carried to fill the demands of those ever-open mouths in the nest.

Finally the day came when they lined them up and one by one the babies flew. At first they hesitated and hung back until they were nudged out of the nest. Then, they swooped up and down like an early prop plane gone out of control. They exhausted themselves flapping their wings. Some set down in makeshift landings that were unbelievable. Others perched precariously near the danger of cats and barking dogs, but the mother never budged. She just watched and observed, her snappy, black eyes never missing a move. Day by day the birds flew more, flew better, and flew farther until the day came when they were all ready to take their place in the sky with the parents.

I thought of my friends and I remembered the ones who were as wise as the robin. They too nudged their youngsters out of the nest, and then the youngsters sprouted their own wings and led the way. They emerged from a cocoon existence of peanut butter and naps into great beautiful butterflies. The sound of the school bell was like V-E Day to them. They assumed leadership, developed, and grew into active citizens in the community, unearthed talents that surprised everyone (including themselves), and set about restoring order to their lives and rejuvenating their own appearance.

The bus? It's here so soon. Before I've scarcely had time to get my bearings. There he comes hopping off the step and yelling excitedly, "I passed!" It's such a small bus. Why would they send such a small bus for such a group of big, boisterous boys? Or could it be . . . the same bus they sent this morning and my son just grew a lot?

Maybe we've all done some growing today.

grandma (grand'ma), *n.* The mother of one's father or mother.

THE ROLE of a grandmother has never been really defined. Some sit in rockers, some sky dive, some have careers. Others clean ovens. Some have white hair. Others wear wigs.

Some see their grandchildren once a day (and it's not enough). Others, once a year (and that's too much).

Once I conducted an interesting survey among a group of eight-year-olds on grandmas. I asked them three questions. One, what is a grandmother? Two, what does she do? And three, what is the difference between a grandmother and a mother?

To the first question, the answers were rather predictable. "She's old (about eighty), helps around the house, is nice and kind, and is Mother's mother or Father's mother, depending on the one who is around the most."

To the second question, the answers again were rather obvious. Most of them noted grandmothers knit, do dishes, clean the bathroom, make good pies; and a goodly number reveled in the fact that Grandma polished their shoes for them.

It was the third question that stimulated the most reaction from them. Here is their composite of the differences between a mother and a grandmother. "Grandma has gray hair, lives alone, takes me places and lets me go into her attic. She can't swim. Grandma doesn't spank you and stops Mother when she does. Mothers scold better and more. Mothers are married. Grandmas aren't.

"Grandma goes to work and my mother doesn't do anything. Mom gives me shots, but Grandma gives me frogs. Grandma lives faraway. A mother you're born from. A grandmother gets married to a grandfather first, a mother to a father last.

"Grandma always says, 'Stay in, it's cold outside,' and my mother says, 'Go out, it's good for you.'"

And here's the clincher. Out of thirty-nine children queried, a total of thirty-three associated the word "love" with Grandma. One summed up the total very well with, "Grandma loves me all the time."

Actually this doesn't surprise me one small bit. On rare

125

occasions when I have had my mother baby-sit for me, it often takes a snake whip and a chair to restore discipline when I get them home.

"Grandma sure is a neat sitter," they yawn openly at the breakfast table. "We had pizza and cola and caramel popcorn. Then we watched Lola Brooklynbridgida on the late show. After that we played Monopoly till you came home. She said when you were a kid you never went to bed. One night you even heard them play 'The Star-Spangled Banner' before the station went off."

"Did Grandma tell you I was twenty-eight at the time?" I snapped.

"Grandma said twenty-five cents a week isn't very much money for an allowance. She said we could make more by running away and joining the Peace Corps. She said you used to blow that much a week on jawbreakers."

"Well, actually," I said grimacing, "Grandma's memory isn't as good as it used to be. She was quite strict and as I recall my income was more like ten cents a week and I bought all my own school clothes with it."

"Grandma sure is neat all right. She told us you hid our skateboard behind the hats in your closet. She said that was dirty pool. What's dirty pool, Mama?"

"It's Grandma telling her grandchildren where their mother hid the skateboard."

"Mama, did you really give a live chicken to one of your teachers on class day? And did you really play barbershop once and cut off Aunt Thelma's hair for real? Boy, you're neat!" They looked at me in a way I had never seen before.

Naturally I brought Mother to task for her indiscretion. "Grandma," I said, "you have a forked tongue and a rotten memory. You've got my kids believing I'm 'neat.' Now I ask you, what kind of an image is that for a mother?"

"The same image your grandmother gave me," she said.

Then I remembered Grandma. What a character.

126

In fact, I never see a Japanese war picture depicting Kamikaze pilots standing erect in their helmets and goggles, their white scarfs flying behind them, toasting their last hour on earth with a glass of sake, that I don't think of riding to town with my grandma on Saturdays.

We would climb into her red and yellow Chevy coupe and jerk in first gear over to the streetcar loop where Grandma would take her place in line between the trolley cars. Due to the rigorous concentration it took to stay on the tracks and the innumerable stops we had to make, conversation was kept to a minimum. A few times a rattled shopper would tap on the window for entrance, to which Grandma would shout angrily, "If I wanted passengers, I'd dingle a bell!"

Once, when I dared to ask why we didn't travel in the same flow of traffic as the other cars, Grandma shot back, "Laws, child, you could get killed out there." Our first stop in town was always a tire center. I could never figure this out. We'd park in the "For Customers Only" lot and Grandma would walk through the cool building. She'd kick a few tires, but she never purchased one. One day she explained, "The day I gain a new tire is the day I lose the best free parking spot a woman ever had."

I don't have Grandma's guts in the traffic or her cunning. But I thought about her the other day as I sat bumper to bumper in the hot downtown traffic. "Hey, lady," yelled a voice from the next car, "wanta get in our pool? Only cost a quarter. We're putting odds on the exact minute your radiator is going to blow. You can have your choice of two minutes or fifteen seconds." Boy, Grandma would have shut his sassy mouth in a hurry.

We had an understanding, Grandma and I. She didn't treat me like a child and I didn't treat her like a mother. We played the game by rules. If I didn't slam her doors and sass, then she didn't spank and lecture me. Grandma treated me like a person already grown up.

127

She let me bake cookies with dirty hands . . . pound on the piano just because I wanted to . . . pick the tomatoes when they were green . . . use her clothespins to dig in the yard . . . pick her flowers to make a necklace chain. Grandma lived in a "fun" house. The rooms were so big you could skate in them. There were a hundred thousand steps to play upon, a big eave that invited cool summer breezes and where you could remain "lost" for hours. And around it all was a black, iron fence.

I liked Grandma the best, though, when she told me about my mama, because it was a part of Mama I had never seen or been close to. I didn't know that when Mama was a little girl a photographer came one day to take a picture of her and her sister in a pony cart. I couldn't imagine they had to bribe them into good behavior by giving them each a coin. In the picture Mama is crying and biting her coin in half. It was a dime and she wanted the bigger coin—the nickel— given to her sister. Somehow, I thought Mama was born knowing the difference between a nickel and a dime.

Grandma told me Mama was once caught by the principal for writing in the front of her book, "In Case of Fire, Throw This in First." I had never had so much respect for Mama as the day I heard this.

From Grandma I learned that Mama had been a child and had traveled the same route I was traveling now. I thought Mom was "neat." (And what kind of an image is that for a mother?)

If I had it to do all over again, I would never return to Grandma's house after she had left it. No one should. For that grand, spacious house tended to shrink with the years. Those wonderful steps that I played upon for hours were broken down and rather pathetic. There was a sadness to the tangled vines, the peeling paint, and the iron fence that listed under the burden of time. The big eave was an architectural "elephant" and would mercifully crumble under the ax of urban renewal.

Grandmas defy description. They really do. They occupy such a unique place in the life a child. They can shed the yoke of responsibility, relax, and enjoy their grandchildren in a way that was not possible when they were raising their own children. And they can glow in the realization that here is their seed of life that will harvest generations to come.

september 6 — november 2

don't sweat the small stuff

SEVERAL YEARS AGO I adopted an expression to live by. I don't know where I picked it up, probably from some immortal bard on a restroom wall, but it has worked like therapy for me.

To begin with, I used to be a worrier. I worried about whether or not our patio doors were covered by insurance if they were hit by a polo ball. I worried about that poor devil on television who flunked his nasalgraph test. I worried about Carol Channing going bald. I worried about who would return our library books if my husband and I both "went to that great split-level in the sky" together.

When the children were babies, it was worse. I used to get up at night and hold mirrors under their nostrils to make sure they were still breathing. I worried about their spitting out more food than went into their stomachs. I developed a "thing" about germs. When I changed diapers, I washed *their* hands. When we went bye-bye in the car, it was like

133

moving the circus. I had a fetish about the kids drinking their moo-moo from any cup that didn't have their name on it.

Then, along came the thought-provoking slogan, "Don't Sweat the Small Stuff," and my entire life changed.

The things I couldn't do anything about I ignored. The things I could I numbered and filed them in their respective places. I stopped worrying and started relaxing. I quit scaring the kids half to death at night with the mirror routine. I discovered I could pack baby's entire needs for the weekend in a handbag and they could drink out of animal skins if they had to. As for germs, I conducted an experiment one night and found to my delight that a pacifier recovered from a package of coffee grounds in the garbage can rinsed well under hot water and jammed quickly into baby's mouth, actually enjoyed improved flavor.

I quit worrying about Mao Tse-tung, the population of India, litterbugs filling up Grand Canyon, and our wading pool becoming polluted. I quit worrying about what would happen to me if I wore white shoes after Labor Day. Before, I rather imagined Saks would fly their flag at half mast. Maybe *Life* magazine would send a reporter-photographer team to follow me about and record the shock of the man-on-the-street. Or maybe Brinkley would use me in one of those amusing little sign-off stories that Huntley pretends he doesn't hear.

It used to be that getting the jump on fashions each season was like running through your lifetime after a train and never catching it, or waking up each morning and discovering it is always yesterday.

It's true. If you want to buy a spring suit, the choice selection occurs in February: a bathing suit, March: back-to-school clothes, July: a fur coat, August. Did I tell you about the week I gave in to a mad-Mitty desire to buy a bathing suit in August?

134

The clerk, swathed in a long-sleeved woolen dress which made her look for the world like Teddy Snowcrop, was aghast. "Surely, you are putting me on," she said. "A bathing suit! In August!"

"That's right," I said firmly, "and I am not leaving this store until you show me one."

She shrugged helplessly. "But surely you are aware of the fact that we haven't had a bathing suit in stock since the first of June. Our—no offense—White Elephant sale was June third and we unload—rather, disposed of all of our suits at that time."

"Are you going to show me a bathing suit," I demanded, "or do I tell everyone that you buy your fitting-room mirrors from an amusement park fun house?"

"Please, madam, keep your voice down. I'll call our manager, Mr. Wheelock, on the phone. (*Lowers voice*) Mr. Wheelock, we've got this crazy woman on the floor who insists upon buying a bathing suit. You heard me right. A bathing suit. I told her that. What does she look like? W-E-I-R-D. She's wearing a pink, sleeveless dress, carrying a white handbag and has (ugh) white shoes. I agree, Mr. Wheelock, but what should I tell her? Very well. (*Louder*) Madam, Mr. Wheelock says since you are obviously a woman of fine taste, we will call you in February when we unpack our first shipment of swim suits. Would you like that?"

Now, normally, I would have jumped up and down pounding my head with my handbag and become quite physical about it. Instead, I simply smiled and said, "Of course I'll return in February when I will personally release a pregnant moth in Mr. Wheelock's fur vault!" I didn't, of course, but with a crazy woman who wears white shoes in August, the salesperson couldn't really be sure, could she?

I quit worrying about removing upholstery labels that said, DO NOT REMOVE LABEL UNDER PENALTY. I quit worrying about

135

the goonie birds becoming extinct and the communists infiltrating Cub Pack 947.

I stopped taking seriously all this nonsense about hand-me-down clothes having a traumatic effect on your children.

I mean, any mother with half a brain knows that children's apparel comes in three sizes: "A little large, but you'll grow," "Just right—so enjoy," and "A little small, so stoop a little."

I think it was last year when we had a rare phenomenon at our house. All the coats were "Just right—so enjoy." By my rough calculations, this event will not occur again in my life span. Now, did the children appreciate the aesthetic beauty of a sleeve that hit smack between the wristbone and the hand, and hems that neither hit midthigh nor dragged behind them like a train? They did not.

"I'll be the only boy in the sixth grade wearing white go-go boots with tassels." "What are you complaining about? I'll be the only patrol boy wearing Cinderella mittens." "You're kidding with this hat. I know I'll grow, but how big can a head get?"

I just rationalized that I was supplying them with a lifetime of laughs. It's a curious tradition, this passing down of clothes within a family. It's the American way, you know. If you're the oldest in the family, you wear new, but you learn early, "Don't tear it, stain it, sweat in it, or drag it across the floor. It's got a long way to go." If you are somewhere in the middle, the attire is a little lighter from constant washings, a little frayed around the buttonholes, and a little smoother in the seat. If you're "the baby," heaven help you. When style was passed out, you weren't born yet. You're in line for the dingy diapers, the sweaters that were washed by mistake in hot water, the pajama bottoms that don't match the tops and the snowsuit that "cost a pretty penny in its day." (No one seems to remember the day *or* the year.)

Traumas! Hogwash! I have never seen people enjoy such

136

unrestrained belly laughs as when they're reminiscing about the hand-me-downs of their childhood. The long underwear tucked inside the shoes so people would think you were wearing your Sunday-best white hose to school. Wearing your mother's boots—the skinny pointed heels—and stuffing the heels with paper. The first snow when kids emerged like patchwork refugees who had just climbed out of a ship's hold.

No, I rather think kids will have to look back kindly on their days of hand-me-downs, for they'll just have to remember with warm, wonderful nostalgia, the year the coats were, "Just right—so enjoy."

I don't worry anymore about whether or not my light bulb goes off in the refrigerator when I shut the door . . . or what my dog thinks about when he sees me coming out of the shower . . . or whether or not de Gaulle wants the Statue of Liberty back.

I even adjusted to the family's nonconformer, the child who is a rebel, a loner, a renegade—the one I'm convinced the hospital gave me by mistake.

Every family has at least one. He's the preschooler with the active thyroid who gets locked in restrooms because he stayed behind to find out where the water went after you pushed down the handle. He's the one who wanders away from home and gets his arm stuck in a piece of construction pipe. He's the one who rejects store-bought toys in favor of taking the registers out and making tunnels out of old oatmeal boxes. He gets more lickings than all the other kids in the family put together.

In school he gets checkmarks for daydreaming, for not being neat, for not working to capacity. It doesn't seem to bother him. In his preoccupation for other things he is unaware that he drives his family crazy, arriving late for dinner every night, wearing his socks and underwear to bed to save time in the mornings, cutting the grass only when he needs money.

137

I used to worry about him a lot. Had he been a genius I'd have been properly awed by it. Had he been a slow learner, I'd have shown due compassion. But to be neither of these things only confused, puzzled, and tried my patience.

I feared for this unpredictable child who was not only out-of-step with the world but whose feet rarely touched the ground. With his insatiable curiosity and hardheaded drive would he beat paths of greatness and discovery, the likes of Winston Churchill or Michelangelo? I wanted to believe that. Or would he find his measure of happiness drifting in and out of this world, living solely off his enthusiasm, imagination, and penchant for living life to its fullest?

Then one day I saw him clearly in the lines of Henry David Thoreau. He wrote, "If a man does not keep pace with his companions, perhaps it is because he hears a different drummer. Let him step to the music which he hears."

I quit beating my drum for conformity and listened to his beat for a while. His pace was a bit more relaxed, the order of his schedule a bit different. For example, watching a caterpillar cross the driveway took precedent over taking a bath. Finishing a pair of homemade stilts preceded dinner. The awe of discovering newborn robins in the spouting beat reading about Columbus discovering America.

I was not aware of how "far out" I had traveled with his drums until the other day. I was in the process of interviewing a woman to spend a few days with the children while my husband and I went out of town.

As we talked, my nonconformer entered the room. Now, had he been a usual child he would have been holding a conventional water tumbler filled with water. As it was he had seen fit to fill an old-fashioned glass with two ice cubes and float a cherry and a slice of orange on top of it. Did I panic? I did not. I took a deep breath, smiled at my horrified visitor, and said, "I don't sweat the small stuff anymore."

138

To which she gasped, "You mean with a kid drinking in the afternoon the stuff gets bigger?" and bolted for her car.

Oh well, she wouldn't have lasted around here two days.

A Man and His Car

I SHOOK MY HUSBAND AWAKE out of a sound sleep. "I've had that bad dream again," I said.

He yawned, "What bad dream?"

"The one where Lady Bird Johnson comes knocking at our door and asks us to get rid of those junk cars in our driveway."

"Didn't you tell her we're still driving them?" he asks sleepily.

"Yes. Then she looked very concerned and said we should apply for federal funds. She said those rusty heaps in front of our house have set her beautification program back ten years and that no matter what our politics we should care about our country. Then, she just faded away."

139

"That sounds like a nice idea."

"Wake up. We've got to talk about those cars. They're eyesores. We should replace one and I think it ought to be yours."

"Nonsense," he grumbled, "I just spent an entire Saturday touching up the rust spots with black paint."

"On a mouse-gray body, that's hardly a secret," I snarled. "It looks so garish with all those stickers on the rear window, SEE ROCK CITY, BUY LIBERTY BONDS, NRA. Why don't you scrape some of them off?"

"Because they're holding in the rear window." He yawned again.

"I'll bet it was that rusty tailpipe that caught her attention. We could wire it up off the ground."

"Okay, tomorrow take a little wire off the door handles and wire up the tailpipe. You can reinforce the running boards if you want to."

"Yeah, and I might shine up the chrome around the headlights and get a new set of wicks for them. That'll spruce things up a bit."

"While you're at it, why don't you spend a little time on *your* car? It's not exactly a Grand Prix entry, you know."

"Well, I haul twenty or thirty kids a week around in it. What do you expect?"

"All I know is, the insurance company wouldn't insure it. They just sent us a survival kit. Those springs in the seats are exposed so badly if you weren't buckled in with seat belts, you'd be driving from the roof. There's no door on the glove compartment, the rear window won't go up or down, and you have to turn on the radio with a pair of pliers. And who in heaven's name scratched 'Official 500 Pace Car' on the door? You know the best thing we could do for Lady Bird would be to erect a billboard in front of both of them."

"She suggested that," I said quietly.

140

"Then it's settled," he sighed, pulling up the covers. "Now will you turn off the light and let me go to sleep?"

I ignored him and reached in the headboard bookcase for something to put me to sleep. I thought I had made a wise choice. It was one of those books that lists surveys and studies conducted by industries and researchers to find out what motivates people to buy as they do. For example, I discovered that people buy home freezers because they are emotionally insecure and need more food than they can eat. Then I bolted upright. There in front of me was a chapter on what motivates men to buy the cars they do. It said researchers found when dealers put a convertible in their show windows men flocked to look at it. But they invariably bought a sedan. Why?

Psychologists who studied the problem came up with the fact that convertibles were symbolic mistresses. They were flashy. They brought out the eyeballs. They attracted attention. Men looked at them longingly, dreamed a little, lusted a lot. But, in the end, man's common sense, his practical side, his down-to-earth rationalization, told him it was not for him and he bought the sedan. The sedan represented the symbolic wife, the plain, safe girl who would be a substantial mother to his children.

As one "practical sedan" to another, I don't mind telling you this bothered me. Especially, when I began thinking back to the women—er, cars my husband had picked out in the past.

Our first car—which he obviously identified with me—was a secondhand, plain, drab-looking, black you-know-what with a broken window—on my side—and a glove compartment door that sprung out in your lap every time the motor turned over, plus a small printed note on the fender that read, "Please, Don't Kick the Tires."

It was good, clean transportation despite the fact it was an obvious alcoholic and couldn't pass a service station without stopping for a slug of gas with an oil chaser. It was hot in the summer and cold in the winter and asthmatic all year round.

Our first new car, in 1951, indicated I still had not changed. It was as proper as a hearse—no chrome, no extras, and no nonsense. I don't think any self-respecting tiger would have been caught dead climbing into its tank!

We bought another new car in 1955. Only the color and the mortgage balance changed.

I slipped out of bed and peered through the window. Suppose men really picked cars like they picked wives. Was this a car to have an affair with? Was this the jaunty sports cap, silk scarf flying crazily in the wind type of car? Was this a mistress, or a mother in sturdy, sensible sneakers?

In the driveway was our small cheapie foreign car that boasted it never changed body styles year after year. The pitiful bit of chrome on the bumper was rusted from the salt on the streets in winter, and a paper towel was stuffed around the windshield because the thermostat was broken and the heat was intense. The color was mouse gray.

I shook my husband awake. "Let's go out and buy a new

car tomorrow. Something impractical. Something wild. It's important to me."

"Are you crazy?" he groaned sleepily. "Why, I've got too much money tied up in that old heap to let her go. She's good till the fuel pump goes. Besides, she's comfortable."

"That's a rotten thing to say to anyone," I sobbed and went to sleep.

I suppose I'd still have that mouse-gray image in the driveway today if it hadn't been for the garbage truck that plowed into me. As I told my husband when I returned his car minus two fenders, two headlights, and a trunk lid, "That tears it. This car is Hitler's Revenge and it must be replaced. I can't drive a car I can't communicate with."

"If I've told you once I've told you a hundred times," he said, "the car doesn't understand a word of English. It responds only to German commands."

"I tried that," I said. "I saw this garbage truck begin to back up and I said, 'Das ist ein garbage truck, lunkhead, let's get out of here.'"

"What happened?"

"Nothing happened. It just sat there like a stick until the truck hit us. I tried blasting the horn and it peep-peeped like it was apologizing. Incidentally, the horn broke off in my hand. It's in the glove compartment."

"Then what happened?"

"I ran out of German, that's what happened. The truck still didn't know I was back there and started at me again. I tried every German word I knew: glockenspiel, pumpernickel, Marlene Dietrich. I even sang two choruses of 'O Tannenbaum.' That's when the second impact hit. That did it. I whacked it on the instrument panel and said, 'Du bist ein cheapie, that's what you are. One more hit and we're going to look like a crock of sauerkraut.' Just about that time the driver got out of his truck and said, very surprised, 'I thought I hit a bump in the road.' How's that for humiliation!"

143

"Don't worry. I think we can fix her up," said my husband. "Fix her!" I shouted. "You wouldn't dare. Not after what she's put me through. Just think of the merits of a big car. No more shinnying into the seat like a snake into a sleeping bag. No more mud goggles on rainy days. No more massaging your cold feet and shifting gears at the same time.

"Think what it would be to pass cars on a hill. And to ride with your legs outstretched, instead of in a foetal position. Just imagine. We could talk to a car in English. No more having to say, 'By the way, what is it you say when you want the car to go in reverse?'"

"Mutter, bitte," he said.

"Which means?" I sighed wearily.

"Mother, may I?"

"It figures. Tomorrow, we buy a new car."

I never realized it before, but there's an umbilical cord connecting a man to his car. It is perhaps the most possessive, protective, paternal relationship you'll ever encounter. Bound together by a thirty-month loan contract, their hearts beat as one until the car goes back on the lot and is exchanged for a new model to which he transfers his love and affection.

The book was right, of course. He eased onto the seat of the sports car in the show window, his arm slipping ever so slyly over the back of the seat. He caressed the steering wheel and the visor with a gentleness I had never seen before. (I thought I saw him pinch the directional lights.) Then he took a deep breath of resignation, walked over to the conventional model and sighed, "We've got the children to consider."

I was pleased to note my image had improved considerably. It had a radio that didn't take ten minutes to heat up. It had power steering and power brakes. And the color was a deep purple. (Which my husband noted matched the veins in my nose.)

Then I went too far. One night I asked to borrow his car.

144

You'd have thought I wanted to borrow his dental plates to eat caramels.

"Isn't there any other way you can get to card club?" he asked.

"Yes," I replied. "I could tape peanuts to my arms and maybe attract enough pigeons to fly me there, but I'd rather drive the car."

Reluctantly he walked me to the door. "You have your license? Your key ring? Extra money? Witnesses?"

I grinned. "I don't want to marry it, just drive it to card club."

"You have to understand about this model," he explained patiently. "She starts cold. Now some cars need pumping. Don't pump her. *She hates to be pumped!* Get that? All you do is ease the choke out about a quarter of an inch. Then push the accelerator all the way to the floor and just ease up on it a bit. Okay? Not too fast. At the same time, turn the key and gently now, slide the choke back in."

Given the least kind of encouragement—like keeping awake—he also delves into "baby's sluggish crankcase, her puny pistons, her fouled plugs, and her dulling points."

As I slid into the seat, he let fly his last arrow. "Don't gun it and you'll make it."

I turned off the motor. "Don't gun what and I'll make it where?"

"Don't gun the motor and you'll make it to the gas station. The tank says empty, but I know there's enough to coast you in, especially if you make the light on the corner and roll the last fifty feet. Oh, and if it keeps dying on you there are emergency flares in the trunk."

A man and his car—he loves and cherishes it from the first day forward, for richer for poorer, for better or for worse, in sickness and in health, and if Detroit ever turns out a model that sews on buttons and laughs at his jokes, ladies, we're in trouble!

145

The Watercress and Girdle Group

THE NAME OF THE GAME is clubwork.

It's played from September through May by thousands of women who spend billions of volunteer hours every year deciding whether to put kidney beans or whole tomatoes in the Circle Meeting chili, or whether to spray-paint the pipe cleaners for the PTA Easter luncheon pink or purple.

Some women readily recognize the overorganization, the tedious details, the long drawn-out devotion to three-hour meetings. But they rationalize that the real cause is worth it. Other women become impatient with sloppy leadership, dull monologues, and that "why-do-today-what-you-can-talk-about-for-three-more-hours-next-Wednesday" syndrome.

Clubwork is therapy for a lot of women. It gets them into their girdles and out among people. It gives them something else to think about besides how to disguise leftovers and how to get crayon stains out of a shirt pocket that has gone through the dryer. Let's face it. The government couldn't

146

afford to buy the services that come out of women's groups if it cashed in the President and all his holdings.

I like clubwomen. Some of my best friends are clubwomen. I even took one to lunch last week. Some I like better than others. Program chairmen, for example. I have always had a soft spot in my head for them. Those of us in the business of giving speeches have concurred unanimously that program chairmen rate a special place in heaven, where the sun always shines, birthdays cease to show after the age of thirty-three, and John Mason Brown sits at their right hand.

Of all the offices on the duty roster, possibly none is more underrated than the woman who must entertain the membership during an entire club year. For audience variety, she has the elder pillars of the club who attend once a year on Founder's Day and who are too proud to wear their hearing devices. ("The speaker was a sweet little thing, but she mouthed her words.") She has the strait-laced group who objected vigorously when a speaker reviewed *The Scarlet Letter*. ("That hussy! She treated it like a piece of costume jewelry!") She has the new bloods who are pressuring her into arranging a "wine tasting" program. ("Preferably *before* the business meeting, honey.")

While the rest of the membership and the officers spend a quiet summer, the program chairman never sleeps. Oh, the president spends a few anxious evenings rolling and tossing and making plans to have her appendix taken out early in September so she can relinquish the gavel to the vice president.

There's the vice president looking suspiciously at the president whom she suspects is not above having her appendix out to get out of the job of president.

There's the recording secretary in a state of numbness, as she has only attended one meeting as a guest before they elected her to the office. There's the corresponding secretary, who is three years behind in a letter to her mother, wondering how all this is going to work out. And there's the be-wildered treasurer, who is setting her husband up as a pigeon for the club's books in the fall.

Not the program chairman. She is haggling with a department store to stage a free fashion show for women with large thighs. She is buzzing the "hot line" to her president every two days with cries of "I can't get Arlene Francis for twenty dollars . . . shall I try for Betsy Palmer?" She is fighting the battle of personages on vacations, unlisted phone numbers, and speakers who won't commit themselves beyond next weekend.

And she is probably anticipating a scene typical of the one I was involved in recently when the program chairman said brightly, "Marcia, you haven't been to one of our meetings in a long time. I'm sure it's due to the popularity of our speaker, Mrs. Bombeck." To which Marcia looked annoyed and snarled, *"Bombeck!* Good Lord, I thought someone said *Steinbeck* was coming!"

Another clubwoman for whom I have great empathy is the perennial Chairman of the Bazaar. Here is a small lump of helplessness who couldn't say no. Molded by flattery and strengthened by self-confidence, she is put adrift in a sea of home-baked bread and knitted toilet tissue covers.

I know of what I speak. Several years ago I was a bazaar chairman. The doctor tells me in time I may be able to hear a telephone ring without becoming incoherent. I wish I could be sure.

One of the first things a bazaar chairman must adjust to is what happened to all the well-wishers who, only a week ago, hoisted you to their shoulders, marched you around the gym, and sang, "For She's a Jolly Good Pigeon." Their generous offers of "I'll donate thirty quarts of my famous calf's-foot jelly" and "Leave the raffle tickets to me" now sounds like, "Are you kidding? This has been a nothing year for calves' feet" and "Honey, I couldn't sell an inner tube to a drowning man."

In desperation, a bazaar chairman will eventually take on the guise of a Mafia moll, stopping at nothing to "firm up" her committees. I've heard ruthless threats behind the coffee urn that would make your hair stand on end. "All right, Eloise, you take that White Elephant chairmanship or the entire world will know you've got a thing going with your son's orthodontist. I'm not bluffing either. And you just never mind why Jeannie Crabitz took the fish pond. That's between the two of us."

The families of bazaar chairman are also affected by this new-found diversion. Plaintive pleas of "Daddy, when is Mommy coming home for a visit?" are often answered with a sour, "She has to come home on Wednesday—it's the night she defrosts our dinners for the week."

As the bazaar draws near, the fever increases while the house takes on all the physical properties of urban renewal. "I can't sleep," complains her husband, staggering into the living room. "My bed is full of plastic cigarette holders and Hawaiian leis."

"Well, stack them in the closet," she says tiredly.

"What!" he snaps, "and disturb the goldfish that are stacked on top of the stuffed poodles and the Japanese fans?"

The last two days before the bazaar are the wildest. With a lot of luck, the raffle prizes will have been delivered to another state . . . the kitchen committee resigns en masse, resolving only to speak to one another in church on Sundays . . . and there's a strong possibility Santa Claus may not "dry out" in time to make the scene for the kiddies.

Each phone call brings a new trauma: "She insists on donating a size forty-eight angora pullover and I refuse to have it in my booth" . . . "My pickles were solicited for the Country Store booth and if the kitchen wants some, let them do their own telephoning" . . . "I will not have my pitch and

149

throw game in the schoolroom. Last year we broke the blackboard and I had a migraine for a week."

When the last bit of popcorn is swept from the gym and the blackboard repaired and the angora pullover en route to the "missions," some poor, unsuspecting newcomer is bound to remark, "It was a lovely bazaar."

She doesn't know it yet, but that lump of innocence is next year's bazaar chairman.

One of the most overzealous groups of clubwomen I know are the Garden Clubbers. They cannot comprehend that some of us are born into this world to plant glad bulbs upside down. Some of us are resigned to a life without manure and mulch. And that when some of us have a green thumb, it's a skin condition.

Don't misunderstand me. I have nothing but respect for Garden Club women. Especially after the episode my mother and I endured with the dried weeds project. We just couldn't imagine there being much skill to throwing clumps of fall foliage into a pot!

"Why, they must think we're a couple of rubes who just blew into town with the egg money," Mother said. "Imagine! Paying $7.95 for a pot of dried milk pods, a few pine cones, and a couple of sticks with berries on them. We could fill a bathtub with this stuff for forty-nine cents of spray paint."

Maybe it was the vision of a floral-filled bathtub that prompted us to do it. Looking back, we like to think one of the kids left the cap off the glue and we inhaled enough to make us fly. At any rate, the next weekend found Mother and me hacking our way through the woods like Jon Hall and Sabu.

Cattails, we discovered, flourished only in swamps where the bog was knee-high. The prettiest leafy specimens were always at the top of the trees. The most unique pods were always situated in the middle of a livestock relief station.

150

And the most graceful Queen Anne's lace was always over the next hill.

I have no intention of humiliating my mother by relating that grim scene of her up to her knees in jungle rot, clutching a bundle of poison sumac to her chest and shouting hysterically at a snake slithering over her gym shoes. (Only to report that she shouted to the heavens, "Oh please! I'm Evangelical and I tithe!")

I think our little excursion can best be told by a tabulation we compiled of the expenses incurred in the pursuit of dried stock for floral arrangements.

Expenses

1 can gold spray paint	$ .69
1 can silver spray paint	.69
1 gallon paint thinner	1.25
(Used to remove spray paint from patio floor)	
1 ironing board cover	2.00
(Note to amateurs: put the leaves *between* wax paper before pressing)	
1 pair gym shoes	4.00
1 sweater (Abandoned at snake pit)	5.95
1 car wash and vacuuming	2.00
1 doctor (for sumac)	5.00
1 prescription (for sumac)	3.57
1 overdue book on *Dried Flowers for Fun and Profit*	.62
Personal Aggravation	500.00
TOTAL	$525.77

It's not that I don't appreciate Garden Clubbers' talents, it's just that they are always trying to convert you to Gardenism. One enthusiast, in particular, bugs me all the time. She's always pinching my brown leaves off my indoor plants and feeling the soil around my pots to see if they've been watered lately. She makes me nervous.

151

"What did you do with that slip of creeping phlox I gave you?" she asked the other day.

"It crept into the soil and died," I said.

"If I've told you once," she sighed, "I've told you a thousand times plants are like little people. You simply have to give them a little water, a little love, and a lot of understanding. Now, this is lovely and green. What do you call this?"

"I call that a rotten onion that has been around for nine weeks and is pithy and mushy on the inside, but has bright green sprouts on the outside."

"You're terrible. You really are," she chided. "You should belong to a Garden Club. Then you could exchange ideas and learn from the other members."

"I belong to the 'Wilt and Kill,'" I offered.

"The 'Wilt and Kill'?" she asked her eyes widening. "I don't think I know it."

"We're a group of Garden Club rejects . . . meet the first rainy Monday of the month . . . answer roll call with our current houseplant failure."

"You're putting me on."

"No, I'm not. It's not too easy to qualify. One girl used a nine-foot sunflower plant as a border. She got in. Another padded her beds with plastic flowers from the dime store . . . in the winter. She qualified. I call every flower Semper Fidelis. It's the only Latin I know. I'm an officer."

"Incredible. I've never heard of it."

"We have a wonderful time. At the last meeting Maybelle Mahonia set up the projector and showed home movies of her garden. It was as barren as a missile site. We got a prize for every weed we could identify. Would you like to hear our slogan?"

"I don't think so," she said, feigning dizziness.

"It's 'From Futility to Fertility We Stand Together.'"

152

"Oh dear. I must be going. Incidentally, how is your sweet potato vine?"

I smiled. "It was delicious."

Ah clubwork . . . the escape hatch from the land of peanut butter and the babblings of children. If it bothers you that so much leadership ability is dormant somewhere, not because of apathy, but because these women don't want to pay the price of boredom to do the job, you could lure them back into the meeting halls easier than you think.

1. Pick a leader because she's a leader, not because she owns the punchbowl and the folding chairs.

2. Frisk all grandmothers and new mothers at the door for snapshots of children. (Check knitting bags, bras, garters, and umbrellas.)

3. Forget the democracy bit. Run the meeting like a railroad or you'll never get home in time to thaw the hamburger.

4. When ankles swell and handbag handles cause red marks to streak up the arm, adjourn the meeting.

5. Plan brief, meaningful meetings and get something done. I wouldn't be surprised if capable women beat a path to your mousetrap!

While You're Down in the Dumps . . .

WHEN MY HUSBAND AND I appear at an antique show there is a scurrying of feet while one dealer whispers to another, "Stick a geranium in that slop jar, Irving, here comes a couple of live ones."

This is partly our fault. We stand there openmouthed and bug-eyed, clutching green cash like we just hit town long enough to buy the fertilizer. On at least one occasion I have rushed over to a large hulk of metal and shrieked, "Is this a 1900 milk separator?" "No," someone replies patiently, "that's a 1962 drinking fountain."

We have maintained a rule of thumb. If you can sleep on it, plant flowers in it, frame it, play it, eat it, stuff it with magazines, records or blankets, ring it or open a conversation with it, we'll buy it.

Then we have an open category of things we're going to do something with some day. This takes in a cast-iron angel with a broken foot, a hand-driven child's washing machine, a Civil War grave marker, and a collection of "Go with Willkie" campaign buttons.

In Maine one summer we picked up a faded, musty chessboard for two dollars. It hung in our garage like a conscience for two years before my husband painted it bright red, mounted it on a turntable, and called it a "lazy susan for gracious eating." "This is going to revolutionize our eating habits," he said. "No more bloated stomachs from waiting for the kids to pass the food. No more flesh wounds from knife cuts and fork pricks. No more unnecessary conversation at the dinner table." He put the lazy susan on the table, placed our food on it, and whirled it. It looked like a fattening roulette wheel. "The success of this device," he went on, "can be summed up in two words: *keep alert*. When the turntable stops at your plate, take whatever is in front of you. You will have eight seconds to spear or spoon the food to your plate. We cannot make exceptions. I'll blow a whistle and the turntable will move again. This way in thirty-two to forty seconds we will all have our plates loaded with hot food and ready to eat. Get it?"

We got it. The first night the food was not placed in its proper order and we had whipped potatoes *over* gravy and strawberries *under* shortcake. The "whistler" promised us this would be remedied at the next meal. Then, we had the problem of overhang. That is, a coffee pot handle, a large plate or an onion ring strategically placed could conceivably clip the glasses or cups and throw the entire timetable off schedule by as much as four or five seconds.

154

It was time for another lecture. "All right, group, I've noticed this time your performance was a little ragged. You spoon drippers and bowl clangers all know who you are. No need to mention names. Now, let's put our shoulders to the wheel and shape up!"

Within two weeks, I noticed some drastic changes. I was five pounds lighter and—due to the centrifugal force whirling around before my eyes at mealtime—I was hopelessly hooked on Dramamine.

I did what any mother would do—I stole his lousy whistle!

Other antiques we bought were equally popular. A dear little 1809 collapsible rocker attacked the baby when he tried to sit in it and he's avoided it like a penicillin shot ever since.

The pump organ that was to bring togetherness to our brood also brought disharmony to the family circle. But how do you tell this to a man who has just displaced a disc and two old friends lugging it into the hallway?

Add to that a bill for $140 to replace the reeds and keep its bellows from becoming asthmatic and you've got a pretty good argument for sentiment.

155

"Where are we going to put it?" I asked.

"Think of it," he said, "a bowl of popcorn, a basket of juicy apples, and all of us locked arm in arm singing, 'Kentucky Babe.' Doesn't that just make your flesh crawl?"

"I'll say. Where are we going to put it?"

"I still remember a chorus or two of 'There's a Fairy in the Bottom of My Teacup.' If you promise not to drown me out, I might let you read poetry in the background on Sundays."

"We can't leave it here in the hallway. It's on my foot."

"And home weddings," he rambled. "Think of it, with a vase of . . . what are those flowers at weddings?"

"Orange blossoms, and get this thing off my foot!"

The organ, with all its scrolls, ornate panels, carpeted pedals, and elevated candle holders, was christened "The Heap" and was placed in the living room. Its stay here was a short one. Guests complained the organ, the candles, and the flowers were a little much and gave them a creepy feeling. (The fact that the only song my husband knew with two hands was "The Old Rugged Cross" didn't help things either.) "The Heap" was reassigned to our bedroom. Here, it became a living tabernacle for unpaid bills, unanswered letters, ties that needed cleaning, old road maps, car keys, and odd bits of change. Occasionally we'd crack our shinbones on it, which prompted us to move it to the family room. It lasted there two days. A cry of dissension went up among the young television viewers who were forced to read lips over the roar of the foot pedals and the gasps of the bellows. The next stop was the porch solarium where "The Heap" developed a decided wheeze in her bellows from the moisture. She came to rest in the kitchen.

Our problem is twofold. Serving five people seated around a pump organ and living in constant fear of a spontaneous chorus of "There's a Fairy in the Bottom of My Teacup."

Very frankly, it is next to impossible to instill respect in

156

small children for antique furniture. Cries of "Get your feet off that distressed table!" or "Don't sit on that woodbox, it could go any minute," leaves them confused and mumbling, "She's got to be kidding."

At roadside shops on Sundays, they make snide remarks about "all this junk" and end up buying a bag of hoarhound candy which they immediately discover they hate and spit out in my hand.

Those of us who don't have Early Grandmothers with attics, or an "in" with a dealer who reads the obituaries daily, must come by antiques the hard way, via the dump.

My affinity for dumps dates back further than my affinity for antiques. As a child, I lived three blocks from a Discount Dump. It was outside the high-rent district and it was every man for himself. I could canvass that dump in fifteen minutes in my bare feet, taking in every seatless wicker chair, canning jar carton, and soiled lampshade.

When we were married, the dump seemed a logical place to accessorize our home. Of course, I'm not attracted to all dumps. Certainly not the status dumps. They have their own curator. They're no fun at all. The curator lives in a small shack and spends his days cleaning and stacking old bricks, boxing sundry tools for easy inspecting, putting cast-offs in some kind of order and reading *House Beautiful.*

He usually greets you at the car with a brisk "May I help you?" When you say, "No, I'm just browsing," he follows along closely at your elbow, pointing out how that rusty auto crankcase would make an adorable planter for a solarium or how that little bamboo birdcage was owned by one bird in East Brunswick who slept a lot.

Other dumps are literally for the birds. Last summer in New England, for example, our garbage was becoming a conversation piece. Also, a health hazard. It was packaged and laid wall to wall throughout the kitchen, dining room, and half of the living room. When I asked a neighbor about it, she said, "You mean you haven't seen the dump? You have to go there yourself to believe it. Also to get rid of your garbage."

"*To the dump!*" I shouted wild with excitement.

"What are we going to buy?" asked one of the kids.

I ignored him. Why hadn't I thought of going to a dump in New England. It was probably lousy with Americana—Revolutionary troops marching over the wasteland dropping sabers by the dozens, pewter cups, personal letters to General Washington, signet rings—I could hardly contain myself.

We drove around a long, dusty road until finally we saw more seagulls than we had seen in the travel folders. So this was where they hung out! No sabers, no pewter cups, no antique goodies at all, just garbage. We backed up the car and started to unload. "What are we going to buy?" a small voice persisted. "I saw a rat," said another. "Of all the parents in the world, we had to get the funny ones," snarled the other one.

No matter. I will go on sewing my heirloom quilts on hot summer days and collecting old hatpins. They're lethal-looking, but they're marvelous for releasing the lock on the bathroom door when someone gets locked in. How the kids will divide all those Willkie buttons when they grow up is their problem.

"Mums the Word for Dad"

THE NEWS that the television networks are telecasting a record number of football games again this season is being met with some violent reactions from housewives across the country.

A few women in the Peaceful Acres development in Connecticut smashed television screens with broom handles. A group of California housewives focused national attention on the problem with their "Psychiatric Drive-Ins" open twenty-four hours a day during the football season. The most notable effort was a group from Virginia who heaved a football through Lady Bird Johnson's window with a terse message, "Would you want your daughter to spend a weekend with one?"

I talked briefly with a group of Ohio women. "It isn't the several hundred games we object to," said the spokesman. "This is only the beginning. Add to that the state and the local games and you've got ten or twelve football games being aired each day of the weekend. Roughly this amounts to one husband propped up in a chair like a dead sponge surrounded by bottle caps."

Heaven knows, men aren't the more talkative of the species. In fact, I have just come by some statistics that claim men average no more than six words a day in their own homes. Furthermore, their only hope of increasing this total is through conscientious massage of the throat muscles.

Even out of football season, men approach their homes in the evening with all the detachment of a census taker. He garages the car, feels the stove to see if there's anything going for him, changes his clothes, eats, and retires to the living room where he reads the newspaper and engages in his nightly practice of finer isometrics—turning the television dial. He remains in a state of inertia until the sound of his deep, labored breathing puts the cork on another confetti-filled evening.

The frustration of wives who want to talk with someone who isn't teething is pitiful. While some accept the silent evenings as a way of life, others try desperately to change it. When one woman attempted to apologize at the dinner table for the children—who were performing a native tribal dance through the mashed potatoes—her husband looked up sharply from his plate, glanced at the children, and shrieked, "You mean they're all ours?" (five words)

One of the most disappointing attempts at starting a conversation is, "What kind of a day did you have, dear?" One husband reportedly answered by kicking the dog, another went pale and couldn't form words, another bit his necktie in half. Some just stared blankly as if they hadn't heard the question. Only one man formed a verbal reply. It was "Shut up, Clara."

Other women work constantly to raise the odds.

WIFE: Know what we're having for dinner? Braised cue tips with sumac topping, onion balls in sour cream, and a bird of paradise nesting in a floating sea of chicken fat.

HUSBAND: I had it for lunch. (5 words)

WIFE: There's another man, Lester. We're civilized people. Let's talk about it.

HUSBAND: Wait till the commercial. (4 words)

WIFE: I broke my leg last week, Wesley. I was waiting for you to notice. See how well I'm doing on crutches?

HUSBAND: Get me a cold one while you're up. (8 words, but he was stoned)

"With the football season it's worse," said a small blonde. "My husband sits down at eight o'clock on a Friday night and never takes his eyes off the screen. I say to him, 'You wanta eat now, Ed?' and he just sits there. I say to him, 'You comin' to bed now, Ed?' and he just sits there. I said to him the other night, 'The woman is here to buy the kids, Ed,' and he didn't move a muscle. I finally took his pulse. It was weird."

"I know what you mean, honey," said a small brunette. "My Fred says to me, 'We need a color TV set. The networks have eighty-three games in color this year.' I said to him, 'If you like to see all that red plasma and those blue bruises, it's okay with me. Frankly, I like to see a man with his front teeth.' He gets real sore. Plugs the high school game into his ear, puts one eyeball on the state game and the other on the National Football League and yells, 'Keep those kids quiet.' We don't have kids."

"If you're thinking of joining them, forget it!" said another voice. "I used to watch football games at college and loved 'em. But on TV. First, I sat through shots of last week's game, then a preview of this week's line-up. When the game finally started, we saw it in live action, then slow motion, then stop action and instant replay. After that we switched to another camera to see if he got a better 'side' of the ball carrier. At the half we had highlights of the first half, followed by interviews of people who chewed over the way they played the first half and predicted what they were going to do the second half. Finally, the game over, we had a recap of the game by the announcer topped off by fifteen minutes of Scoreboard."

"Then what's the answer?" someone asked.

"We fight back with *Peyton Place*," said a newly-wed snapping her fingers with inspiration.

"Here's the deal. We get the network to bring on *Peyton Place* thirty minutes early and watch exciting shots from last week's show, followed by previews of this week's action. Then we have Betty Furness interview Old Man Peyton and his grandson just for a little flavor.

"When the action starts, the camera will replay in slow motion all the scenes, then stop-action all the dirty parts and have an instant replay of all the violent parts. After that, we'd switch to another camera for another view of Betty Cord in her negligee. At the 'break' they'd show action from the first half followed by an interview by Ann Landers, who would chew over the first half and offer advice on how it should be played the second half.

"When the show is over, Dr. Joyce Brothers would tally up

161

the marriages for each, the divorces, the surgery, and their standing in the league."

"It's just got to work," said a quiet brunette. "I'm so desperate, I'm beginning to talk to my kids."

NOVEMBER 3 — JANUARY 1

EAT YOUR HEART OUT, HELOISE!

IT HAPPENS every November. I don't know why. I suffer an attack of domesticity. I want to bustle about in a starched apron, bake bread, iron sheets, and make my own soap. I want to beat mattresses, mend cleaning rags, wax the driveway, and can green beans. I want to dust the coffee table and arrange it with a vase of flowers and a copy of Norman Vincent Peale. In short, I am nauseating.

I call it my "Eat Your Heart Out, Heloise" syndrome. It's like a strange power that overcomes me and lasts no longer than two days. During that span I can hardly remember what I have done or why I have done it. All I know is when I return to my old self, I usually have a pot of ox tail soup brewing and am sitting in my rocker reading, "How to Remove Kite String Marks from the Spouting," and wondering what I am doing here.

Last November's seizure was a doozie. When I returned to

my slovenly ways I discovered I had rearranged the furniture, giving it all the personality of a bus station restroom. Ignoring the advice of experts, I washed the draperies, causing the lining to sag like a toddler's underwear.

I discovered I had gone to town and returned home with twenty yards of red corduroy for bedspreads. Heaven knows what I would have purchased if I owned a sewing machine. They tell me I alerted the entire household, lined them up on the front lawn and insisted we begin fertilizing early for spring, putting in the screens and beating the rugs. I have never viewed such sickening efficiency in my life. The woodwork glistened. The windows sparkled. I had even taken the paper clips out of the tea canister and replaced them with tea.

I have talked with other women about this strange phenomenon and they assure me it is normal. This return to order is sparkled by cool weather, an anticipation of the holidays and a large guilt complex that I shouldn't be enjoying myself so much with the children in school.

I have found that a cold shower shocks me back to my slovenly ways. I know I am slovenly because I gave myself one of those magazine quizzes once to find out if I was "children-geared," "husband-geared," or "house-geared."

The "child-geared" mother often referred to her husband as what's-his-name and took a tape recorder to the labor room to record her suffering so she could play it at her children's weddings. I wasn't that. A "husband-geared" woman fed her husband steak and the kids hamburger. I wasn't that. A "home-geared" woman fixed up the basement for the family to live in and cried whenever someone splashed water on her kitchen tiles. I wasn't that.

According to my score, I wasn't crazy about any one of the three. In fact, in homemaking I only scored five out of a possible hundred points. (I changed the paper in my birdcage with some kind of regularity.)

What makes this confession so incongruous is that fifteen years ago, I did a three-times-a-week newspaper column on housecleaning. As I remember it, one day I slipped out of my office for just a moment to go to the coffee machine. When I returned I had been elected by the department as its next homemaking editor. (Incidentally, newspapering is the only profession in the world so full of finks you have to have your own food taster.) In short, I had been had.

I called it "Operation Dustrag" and set about advising the housewives of the city how to develop a positive attitude toward cleaning so they wouldn't become cranky and irritable with their family. I assured them if they stuck with me and my thrice-weekly household cleaning schedule, we could re-store order to their houses and literally tap-dance our way to House Beautiful. (I think I promised them prosperity, an end to World War II, and a cure for the common dustball, but no one got legal about it.)

What really amazed me was how seriously women took their housekeeping chores. To some, it was a way of life. Their plaintive pleas rolled in daily: "How do I clean my alabaster?" (Madam, I didn't know birds got dirty.) "How can I prevent scrub water from running down my arms to my elbows?" (Hang by your feet when you wash the walls.) "Is there a formula for removing chocolate from overstuffed furniture?" (No, but there's one for beating the stuffings out of the little boy who ate the chocolate on the overstuffed furniture.)

After several irate calls from women who had tried my little balls of paraffin in their rinse water to make the chintz look chintzier—one woman said if her curtains had wicks they'd burn right through Advent—I promised my editor I would try these things at home first. My home began to take on all the excitement of a missile at count-down.

I concocted a mixture of wall cleaner that nearly blew our

167

house off the foundation. I tried samples from manufacturers that took the coin dots right out of the kitchen tile. I had so many sample-type gloves, I wore them for everything from cleaning out the dryer lint trap to shaking hands with my husband.

My succinct advice went on day after day.

To make a towel for the children's bath, simply take two towels and monogram each with an F. One F will represent face, the other, feet. Then, simply toss both towels into a corner on the floor. This sounds primitive, but after three days they won't even want to know which F they're using, and at least the towels will always be where they belong, on the floor.

For mildew or musty odor on the shower curtain, simply take a sharp pair of scissors and whack it off. Actually, the more mildew, the more interesting the shower curtains become.

To clean piano keys, try having your children wear chamois gloves moistened with clear water. I daresay their practice sessions won't sound any different and you'll have a clean keyboard.

To remove gum stains, pick off as much gum as possible, then soften by applying egg whites. An egg white stain is better to live with than chewing gum.

A sterilizer that has boiled dry will make an interesting conversation piece on the ceiling over your stove. Small rolls of dust under the bed will entertain small children for hours. (Likewise in-laws, malicious neighbors, and the Board of Health.)

The end of "Operation Dustrag" came as a shock to no one. It was entered in statewide competition under the category "columns." As I sat at the banquet table listening to the names of winners, I was numb. If I won something it was another year of "Help Stamp Out Dirt." If I didn't, I couldn't trust myself to go to the watercooler without drawing some other dreary chore.

168

Needless to say, the column went unnoticed. By Wednesday of the following week, I had been assigned to Society where "the bride walks to the altar on the arm of her father" and other funny things happen.

Several years later when I retired to actually keep house, I discovered the real keyword to housecleaning was incentive. I was a fool not to have realized it before. There had to be a reason for cleaning house. At our place, the motivation seems to center about one word: *party.*

When we can no longer "dig out," we simply announce to twenty or thirty of our most intimate friends, we are going to entertain. Then we swing into action. My husband knocks out a wall or two, gives the baseboards that long-promised second coat, changes the furnace filter, replaces light bulbs where there has been no light for five years, squirts glazing compound into holes and wall cracks, and hot-mops the driveway.

The children are in charge of scouting the sandbox and toy chests for good silverware, hauling away the debris under their beds, disposing of a garbage full of bottles and returning the library books.

I have my own busy work. I discard all the jelly glasses and replace them with "matched" crystal, exchange all the dead houseplants for new ones from the nursery, and of course plan the menu and the guest list.

Our parties have always been memorable. We always have the wet picture frames that someone invariably leans against and has to be cut out of with sharp scissors. We always have the freshly laid fire in the sparkling clean grate and the closed draft that sends our guests coughing into the dark streets. We always have one guest who is rude enough to inquire why our living room wall is sagging and suggests perhaps our attic is a little overloaded.

The "day after party day" then is always designated "Clean

the attic day." Now let me offer this bit of advice. If your marriage is already a little unstable to begin with, forget the attic. We never do, but then we've been written up several times in the *Ladies' Home Journal* feature, "Can This Marriage Be Saved?"

Usually we let down the attic stairs—which the Good Lord knows is enough of a physical strain the day after a party—and we scale the heights together. After considerable effort, my husband speaks, "Let me begin by saying that you can't be illogical or sentimental about this stuff."

"Well, that's pretty pompous coming from a man who still has his Jack Armstrong signet ring, a book of shoe stamps from World War II, and his first bow wow!"

"Those are collector's items," he explains. "That's different. I'm talking about junk. Right now, we are going to establish a rule of thumb for saving things."

We sit down on a carton marked RAIN-SOAKED HALLOWEEN MASKS. "Now," he continues, "if we can't wear it, frame it, sell it, or hang it on the Christmas tree, out it goes! Understand?"

At the end of two hours we haul four pitiful items to the curb: a broken hula hoop, an airline calendar showing Wiley Post spinning a propeller, an empty varnish can, and one tire chain.

"This is ridiculous," he growls, crawling back into the attic. "Let's take this stuff one by one. What's this?"

"That's our summer cabin inventory."

"What summer cabin?"

"The one we're going to buy someday. So far, we have a studio couch, a lamp with a bowling pin base, six Shirley Temple cereal bowls, two venetian blinds, and a chair with a rope seat."

"And this?" he sighs.

"That's my motherhood insurance. They're all my old ma-

170

ternity clothes, bottle sterilizer, potty chair, layettes, baby bed, and car seat. You lay a hand on this stuff and we'll both live to regret it."

"And all this trash?"

"That belongs to you. Consecutive license plates from 1937, old fertilizer bags, a rusted sickle, a picture of the Cincinnati Reds, autographed by Bucky Walters, the medical dictionary wrapped in a plain, brown wrapper, cartons of English quizzes from the class of 1953, eighteen empty antifreeze cans, a box marked 'Old Furnace Filters' and a bait box that is trying to tell us something."

"Okay," he sighs, "I won't raise a finger. Put it out at the curb and call the junk man."

I grinned. *"The junk man.* You've got to be kidding. Gone is the simple, little peddler who used to beat a path to your curb in search of a bushel basket of cast-offs. Gone are the agency trucks who used to be in your driveway before you

171

got the receiver back on the hook. Hustling junk is a real art nowadays."

And I meant it. It had been my experience that if you're stuck with an old swing and gym set, it is easier to start a second family than to try to unload it. If you're saddled with an extension ladder with a couple of rungs missing, hire an adventurous painter with no dependents. As for having a car in the driveway that won't run, fella, that's about as thrilling to move as a dead horse!

On the day the agency trucks go by, I find myself running around the garage like a frustrated auctioneer, spreading my wares out attractively in the driveway and adjusting spots to highlight the plastics. "Boy, have I got goodies for you to-day," I yell. "I've got a set of corn holders, a size-twelve wedding gown worn only once, a box of Mason jars that will drive antique collectors mad, and a carton of coat hangers that are still in their productive years. That is, if you'll take this bed.

"You don't want the bed? Tell you what I'm gonna do. I'll throw in two pairs of ice skates, a garden hose, and a pressure cooker. No deal? All right, sir, you seem like a man of some discernment. As a special offer this week, I am offering your truck first choice on a nearly new beer cooler, thirty-five back issues of *Boy's Life*, and a hand-painted Nativity scene. If you'll take the bed off my hands.

"Really, sir, you do drive a hard bargain. To show faith, I'll tempt fate by giving away my layettes. That is positively my final offer. After all, this bed is a real find. It was only used by a little old lady from Pasadena who had insomnia. What do you mean, who told me that ridiculous story? You did when I bought the bed at your outlet store for ten dollars."

"Your story is touching," said my husband, "but what are we going to do with all this trash?"

I shrugged. "Bring it downstairs and we'll plan our next party."

172

"One More 'Ho Ho Ho' and I'll Paste You in the Mouth"

"WHO CARES if it fits? She takes everything back anyway. Billie Joe, if you get hit by a truck, the next time I'll leave you at home! Why did I wear these boots? It never fails. I wear boots and the sun comes out! Will you please stop pulling at me. I did buy my Christmas cards last January. I just can't find them. Cheap stuff. They always put out cheap stuff at Christmas. Did you see that man shove me? Same to you, fella!

"Don't dilly-dally to look at store windows. I've got all my baking to do, the house to decorate, presents to wrap, the cards to mail . . . mailman! I forgot to get something for the mailman. Boy, everyone's got their hand out at Christmas, haven't they. Well, did you see that? I was here first and she hopped in right in front of me. We oughta get numbers like they do at the butcher counter. That would take care of those pushy ones. Same to you, fella!

"I don't care if the box fits, just any box will do. So don't send it. Let me occupy a whole bus with it. You tell the policeman when I occupy a whole seat that your truck driver couldn't deliver it. Lines . . . lines . . . I'll have to get in line to die . . . Billie Joe, you're too old for the Santa Claus bit. Don't think I don't know why you want in line . . . for a lousy candy cane. You'd stand in line if they were handing out free headaches.

"What music? I don't hear any music. I think I'll just give Uncle Walter the money. He's always liked money. In fact, he's never happy with anything else you give him. And that gift exchange. Wish we could get out of that. I always get something cheap back. My feet hurt. You'd think some man would get off his duff and give a woman a seat. No one cares about anyone anymore. I don't hear any music.

173

"My headache's back. Wish I could take off these boots. I think we're ready to . . . wait a minute, Billie Joe. I forgot Linda's birthday. Doesn't that beat all. It's what she gets for being born on Christmas Day. Now, I've got to run up to fourth floor and fight those crowds all over again. You wait here with the shopping bags and don't wander do you hear? No sense running you all over the place. Boy, some people have a fat nerve having a birthday on Christmas Day. I don't know of anyone who has the gall to be born on Christmas Day. What did you say, Billie Joe?"

"I said, 'I know SomeOne.'"

"Deck the Halls with Boughs of Holly . . ."

MY IDEA OF DECORATING the house for Christmas is to light up the rooftop with bright strings of bulbs, drape garlands of greenery from pillar to post, flash spots of bauble-studded trees, garnish the garage door with a life-sized Santa Claus, and perch a small elf on the mailbox that says "Y-U-L-E" where his teeth should be.

My husband's idea of decorating for Christmas is to replace the forty-watt bulb in the porch light with a sixty-watter.

"You act like I'm against Christmas or something," he said defensively. "Why, no one gets any more excited about the holidays than I do."

"Yeah, we've noticed how emotional you get when all those cars line up and breathless little children point to our house and say, 'Wowie, that's some sixty-watt porch light bulb!'"

"The trouble with you," he continued, "is that you overdo. If you'd just keep it simple. But no! You can't rest until you have me shinnying over the rooftops in a snowstorm with a shorted string of light bulbs in my teeth."

"I don't want to talk about it. You've been crabby ever

174

since you dropped your GI insurance. Heaven knows, it isn't the children's fault."

"What do you want to say dumb things like that for? And where are you going with those bulbs?"

"I am going to hang them on the bare branches of the tree in the front yard."

"I hope they're weatherproof. Remember the year you hung those little silver birds from the branches? I don't think I shall ever forget looking up from my breakfast and seeing those little feathered devils disintegrating before my eyes. It was like watching their intestines unravel."

"You've told that story a thousand times. These bulbs are waterproof."

"Junk . . . nothing but junk!" he said, pawing through the boxes. "I wouldn't be caught dead standing out there in the snow draping this wretched stuff over the trees."

"I know. You're the type who would buy roller skates for Tiny Tim!"

"Do you have a ladder?"

"I don't need one. I'm going to balance a bar stool on the milk box."

"I knew it," he said, "you just couldn't stand to see me sit in here where it's warm. You've got to involve me in your Disneyland extravaganza. All right, we might just as well do the job right. First, I'll make a sketch of the tree and we'll figure out mathematically how many blue, gold, and red bulbs it will take to make it look right."

"You ruin everything," I grumbled. "You and your planning. Did anyone ever tell you you're about as much fun as a fever blister under the mistletoe?"

"I tell you what," he shouted, jumping out of his chair. "Let's keep it simple this year. I'll put a sixty-watt light bulb in the porch light and we'll all stand around and sing, 'Good King Wenceslaus.' You know, I bet I'm the only one here who knows the second stanza by heart . . ."

175

"Up On the Housetop Reindeers Pause . . . Out Jumps Good Old Santa Claus . . ."

IF THERE IS one man singularly responsible for the children of this country, it's Doctor Spock. (That reads strange, but I don't know how to fix it.)

What I'm getting at is, this man is the great white father of every parent who has bungled his way through a vaporizer tent or a two-year-old's tantrum. Why, there was a time when, if Doctor Spock had told me to use one-legged diapers, I would have done so without question.

Now he has shaken me up. He has said there is no Santa Claus and urges us to tell our children the truth.

"Kids, brace yourselves," I said. "Doctor Spock says there is no Santa Claus and that I should never have taken you to see a live one in the first place because his behavior is noisy and his clothes are strange. Also, he inspires greed."

They looked at each other, obviously stunned.

"That's just not true," one said. "You know there's a Santa Claus, just as you believe there are fairies dancing on our lawn."

"Knock it off with the 'Yes, Virginia' bit. I told you that. Now I'm telling you Santa Claus is an upsetting experience. There can't be a Santa Claus."

"There can if you want him to be," they said cautiously.

"I don't know," I hesitated. "He does have a certain magic that makes people happy and kind toward one another. He does keep the work economy steady for elves and gives seasonal employment to reindeer. Heaven knows, he has your father spending more money than he earns and all of us crawling around on the rooftops with strings of lights in our teeth. I don't know what to believe anymore. I've always had such faith in Dr. Spock!"

176

"Have you ever seen Dr. Spock?" asked one.

"No, but . . . now *cut that out!* I know he exists. The point is how can I go on believing in a Santa Claus who parachutes from a helicopter over a shopping center parking lot, breaks his leg and ends up in a hospital?"

"Well, where else would you go with a broken leg?" asked another.

"The point is, kids, he's merely a mortal man, and mortal men don't go around pushing their fat stomachs down skinny chimneys."

"Of course he's mortal," they explained. "Otherwise, how could he have eaten all those cookies you put out for him last year?"

"That's right," I said excitedly, "he really did come, didn't he, and left me that dreamy black jacket that I *know* your father wouldn't have bought. You know something? I believe in Yogi Bear, and his behavior is noisy. I believe in Phyllis Diller and her clothes are strange. I believe in the Bureau of Internal Revenue and they're not exactly philanthropic. Kids, there is a Santa Claus!"

As the curtain closed on this domestic scene, the seven-year-old leaned over to whisper in his father's ear, "Boy, Dad, she gets harder to convince every year!"

Memo to: Mr. Kravitz, principal
From: Katherine Courageous
Re: Christmas Pageant

The Christmas Pageant will be a little late this year. Possibly January 23 if that date is agreeable with you.

Although an enthusiastic Pageant Committee has been at work since October, we have had some problems. To begin with, there were several on the committee who insisted on making a musical out of the Nativity story. At one point, we had the precision drill team making a "B" for Bethlehem in the background while a trio of baton twirlers marched around

177

the stable. This idea was scratched when someone remembered batons hadn't been invented yet.

Remember how excited we were about the donation of a "live" donkey? Our custodian, Mr. Webber, does not share our excitement. Although his phrasing was a little less delicate, he intimated that if the animal was not "gym-floor trained" by January 23, we could jolly well go back to papier-mâché. He also said (this is quoted out of context) that the smell of the beast wouldn't be out of the auditorium in time for the Lions' annual Chili Supper next May.

We have had a few casting problems to plague us. I had to award the Mary, Mother of Jesus, role to Michael Pushy. (His parents donated the donkey.) Michael refused to wear a wig, which might be a little confusing to the audience, but I'll make a special note on the program. I've had great pressure from Mrs. Reumschusser. It seems her son, Kevin, is a Ted Mack loser who plays "Rudolph the Red-Nosed Reindeer" on the spoons. I am using him at intermission.

The costumes didn't arrive until three days ago from the Beelzebub Costume Company of New Jersey. There was obviously an error. Instead of thirty Roman soldier uniforms, there were thirty pink suede bunny leotards with matching ears. It was quite apparent to me that after I had tried a few on our "little people," this was not our order. Miss Heinzie and myself couldn't help but speculate that somewhere there is a tired businessman with a Roman soldier sitting on his lap.

The shop department is not yet finished with the special scaffold for parents wishing to take pictures and tape-record the program. We felt this necessary after Mr. Happenstance's accident last year when he panned in too closely and fell into the manger.

I hate to ask, but could you please do something diplomatic with Mrs. Ringading? She has threatened the refreshments committee with her traditional whiskey balls and rum cookies. You know what a fire hazard they created last year.

In view of the fact that two of our shepherds have diarrhea, we respectfully request the Pageant be postponed until January 23 or after.

178

"God Rest Ye Merry Gentlemen . . ."

THAT CLICKING SOUND you hear about this time is the result of fourteen million husbands pushing the panic button. They are pushing it because they are hours away from Christmas and still have no gift for what's-her-name, mother of his four children.

One of the more conscientious husbands can always be counted upon to come up with the item mentioned last July when his wife snarled, "What I need around this house is a decent plunger!" Inspired by his power of retention he will sprint out and have a plunger wrapped as a gift. No one will be more surprised than he when his wife cups it over his mouth!

Others will seek out the advice of young secretaries who have read all the magazines and know that happiness is an immoral nightgown. Depending upon the type of wife she will (a) return the nightgown and buy a sandwich grill, or (b) smile gratefully and wear it to bed under a coat, or (c) check out the secretary.

179

For the most part husbands are cast adrift in a sea of confusion and bewilderment, sniffing perfumes, fingering sequins, and being ever on the lookout for a woman who looks like his wife's size.

Don't ask me why my heart goes out to these desperate men. Maybe it's that time of year. Maybe it's the den mother in me. Maybe I have really forgotten the rotten gift I found in my stocking last year: a gift certificate for a flu shot! At any rate, some of my women friends have asked me to pass along to men some guideposts to shopping.

First, women are never what they seem to be. There is the woman you see and there is the woman who is hidden. Buy the gift for the woman who is hidden.

Outwardly, women are a lot of things. They're frugal souls who save old bread wrappers and store antifreeze during the summer in the utility room. They're practical souls who buy all black accessories and cut their own hair. They're conservative souls who catch rainwater in a saucepan, and take their own popcorn to the drive-in. They're modest souls who clutch at sofa pillows to cover their exposed knees. Some still won't smoke in front of their mothers. So, they're dependable, brave, trusting, loyal, and true? Gentlemen, take another look.

Hidden is the woman who sings duets with Barbra Streisand and pretends Robert Goulet is singing to her. Who hides out in the bathroom and experiments with her eyes. Who would wear a pair of hostess pajamas if everyone wouldn't fall down laughing. Who reads burlesque ads when she thinks no one is watching. Who would like to feed the kids early without feeling guilty. Who thinks about making ceramics, writing a play and earning a paycheck.

That's all the help I'm going to give you birds. You've got just a few hours to get to know your wife. If you still think she rates a monogrammed chain saw, that's up to you!

There is a wonderful story of Christmas, about a great cathedral whose chimes would not ring until, as the legend goes, the real gift of love had been placed on its altar.

Year after year, great kings would offer up the riches of their land, but the chimes would not ring.

One year, a small waif in a shabby coat entered the great cathedral and proceeded down the long aisle. He was stopped and asked what he could possibly give that kings had not already offered. The small boy looked down and hopelessly examined his possessions. Finally, he took off his coat and laid it gently at the foot of the altar.

The chimes rang.

To receive a gift, molded from love and sacrifice, selected with care and tied up with all the excitement the giver has to offer, is indeed rare. They don't come along often, but when they do, cherish them.

I remember the year I received my first "Crumb Scraper." It was fashioned from half a paper plate and a lace doily. I have never seen such shining pride from the little four-year-old girl who asked, "You don't have one already, do you?"

The crumb scraper defied description. When you used one part of the cardboard to guide the crumbs into the plate, they bounced and scattered through the air like dancing snowflakes. But it didn't matter.

I remember a bookmark created from a piece of cardboard with a picture of Jesus crayoned on the front. It was one of those one-of-a-kind collector's items that depicted Jesus as a blond with a crew cut. Crayoned underneath the picture were words to live by, OH COME HOLY SPURT.

My favorite, though, was a small picture framed with construction paper, and reinforced with colored toothpicks. Staring out at me was a picture of Robbie Wagner. "Do you like it?" asked the small giver excitedly. "I used a hundred gallons of paste on it. Don't put it near heat or the toothpicks will fall off."

181

I could only admit it was beautiful, but why Robbie instead of his own picture. "The scissors slipped and I goofed my picture up," he explained. "Robbie had an extra one."

There were other gifts—the year of the bent coat hanger adorned with twisted nose tissues and the year of the matchbox covered with sewing scraps and fake pearls—and then the small homemade gifts were no more.

I still receive gifts at Christmas. They are thoughtful. They are wrapped with care. They are what I need.

But oh, how I wish I could bend low and receive a gift of cardboard and library paste so that I could hear the chimes ring at Christmas just once more.

I WAITED until the end of the book to tell you why I wrote it.

I figured if you got this far, you might need an answer. If you didn't get this far, it wouldn't make any difference.

It goes back to the first time I saw authoress Faith Baldwin in a full-page magazine ad admonishing, "It's a shame more women don't take up writing." I said aloud, "Ain't it the truth, Faith."

She looked directly at me and said, "If you're a woman who wants to get more out of life, don't bury your talents under a mountain of dishes. Writing will provide a wonderful means of emotional release and self-expression, to say nothing of the extra income. You don't have to go to an office with half your mind on your household, wondering if it rains, did you close the windows. (I liked that.) Even though you are tied down to your home, you can still experience fulfillment."

Faith, you had me pegged, all right. I had been a little bored at home. (A *little* bored. Who am I kidding? I was picking lint off the refrigerator.) So, I began to write about what I knew best: the American Housewife. Very frankly, I couldn't think of anyone in the world who rated a better press.

On television she is depicted as a woman consumed with her own bad breath, rotten coffee, underarm perspiration, and irregularity problems. In slick magazines, she is forever being brought to task for not trying to "look chi chi on her way to the labor room," for not nibbling on her husband's ear by candlelight, and for not giving enough of those marvy little intimate dinner parties for thirty or so.

In cartoons, she is a joke. In erudite groups, an exception.

183

In the movies, the housewife is always the one with the dark hair and the no-bust. Songwriters virtually ignore her. She's the perennial bad driver, the traditional joiner, the target of men who visualize her in a pushbutton world. (All of which are contingent on service repairmen whose promises are as good as the word of Judas.)

If she complains, she's neurotic. If she doesn't, she's stupid. If she stays home with the children, she is a boring clod who is overprotective and will cling to her children till they are forty-eight years old. If she leaves her home to work, she is selfish, ambitious, and her children will write dirty words in nice places.

Faith didn't tell me about the secondhand typewriter that tightened up when it rained or had a "7", an "s", and an "o" that stuck. She didn't tell me how I'd have to set up a table at the end of my bed and how my files would spill over into the bathroom. (The Internal Revenue Service didn't buy it either. They're still questioning my expenditure for a new shower curtain for my office.) She didn't tell me about the kids reading over my shoulder and saying, "What's so funny about that?" or interrupting one of my rare literary spasms to tell me that if you filled a washcloth full of water and squeezed it, it would take fourteen drops to fill your navel.

She didn't tell me about the constancy of a column that makes no allowances for holidays, vacations, literary droughts, or kidney infections.

She just said, "Write about home situations, kids—things that only a woman who stayed at home could write about."

At first, I began writing for one woman. I visualized her as a moderately young woman, overkidsed and underpatienced with four years of college and chapped hands all year around. None of the popular images seemed to fit her. She never had a moment alone, yet she was lonely most of the time. She worried more about toilet training her fourteen-month-old

184

than Premier Chou En-lai. And the BOW (Big Outside World) was almost a fable to her.

After a while I began to visualize other women as I wrote. The woman with no children who made a career out of going to baby showers, the teenagers with wires coming out of their ears, hair cascading over their eyes and looking for the world like hairy toasters, the older woman who gagged every time someone called her a senior citizen, and the career girl who panicked when she saw the return of the dress with waistlines and belts. ("God only knows what I've grown under these shifts for four years.")

Through the columns and through the mails, we shared some common ground together. It was—in essence—group therapy. They'd write, "Honey, do something about your picture. You look like a fifty-year-old woman who has just been told by her obstetrician that she's pregnant!" Or they'd say, "You had to tell the world about my urban renewal living room, didn't you? Are you sure you don't live next door to me?" Sometimes their loyalty knew no bounds. "Erma, you're the only woman I let my husband take to bed with him. (Via the Sunday Section) He says you're like an old friend."

Other readers were not so enamored. "Who do you fancy career girls think you are, sitting in a plush office telling us housewives what it's like?" Or the note from an obvious health fadist, "Lady, you make me sick!"

These women and many more make up this book. They represent a myriad of moods, situations, frustrations, and humor that make up a housewife.

When my son learned that I was writing a book his first reaction was, "It isn't going to be dirty, is it?" I turned to him and said, "Kid, I couldn't get this thing banned in a Christian Science reading room." Then, that began to worry me a bit. Other than a small portion dealing with the sex education of our son in the fourth chapter, I have acted like

185

Sex and the Married Housewife do not live in co-existence with one another.

To be perfectly honest, I didn't know how to handle it. I grew up in an era when sex education was a dirty word. I didn't read *Little Orphan Annie* until I was twelve because Mother thought Daddy Warbucks was a dirty old man. I didn't even know *National Geographic* ran pictures until after I was married. Daddy always cut them out.

I can remember, of course, slipping a book by Kathleen Norris off the shelf and putting it between the pages of *Girl's Life*. The heroine, usually named Hiliary, was "pouty, wild, untamed, spoiled, breathless and rich." She always had sensuous lips. (I thought that meant a fever blister until I was fourteen.) The hero was usually Brad who was stubborn, tough, square-jawed, and who spoke huskily when he made love. My eyeballs fairly popped as I got to the meaty parts where Brad and Hiliary met to embrace. Then, it was always the same. "The fire in the fireplace flickered and died." I don't know how many books I plowed through where "The fire in the fireplace flickered and died," leaving me in a world of ignorance and speculation. I hadn't the foggiest notion what was going on while the fire was going out. So you can blame my omission on Kathleen Norris!

I have purposely not let my husband read the manuscript. With a book without sex in it, I can use all the lawsuits I can get to publicize it.

I could be terribly heroic and say I wrote the book because the American Housewife deserved a new, honest image.

I could be terribly sentimental and say I wrote the book because four men have always told me I could do it when I knew I couldn't. There is James W. Harris, my high school journalism teacher, who first had the kindness to "laugh when I sat down at the typewriter." There is Glenn Thompson, editor of the Dayton *Journal Herald*, who took me out of a utility room and is responsible for any measure of success I enjoy. There is Tom Dorsey, director of Newsday Specials, who took a "flyer" on an unknown writer whose credits consisted of bad checks and grocery lists. And not the least my husband, Bill, who when I cling to his knees and beg for criticism of my work, has the wisdom not to give it to me.

To be honest, however, I will have to admit that I wrote the book for the original model—the one who was overkidsed, underpatienced, with four years of college and chapped hands all year around. I knew if I didn't follow Faith's advice and laugh a little at myself, then I would surely cry.

187